RUDOLF STEINER (1861–1925) called his spiritual philosophy 'anthroposophy', meaning 'wisdom of the human being'. As a highly developed seer, he based his work on direct knowledge and perception of spiritual dimensions. He initiated a modern and universal 'science of spirit', accessible to anyone willing to exercise clear and unprejudiced thinking.

From his spiritual investigations Steiner provided suggestions for the renewal of many activities, including education (both general and special), agriculture, medicine, economics, architecture, science, philosophy, religion and the arts. Today there are thousands of schools, clinics, farms and other organizations involved in practical work based on his principles. His many published works feature his research into the spiritual nature of the human being, the evolution of the world and humanity, and methods of personal development. Steiner wrote some 30 books and delivered over 6000 lectures across Europe. In 1924 he founded the General Anthroposophical Society, which today has branches throughout the world.

ASTRONOMY AND ASTROLOGY

Finding a Relationship to the Cosmos

RUDOLF STEINER

Compiled and edited by Margaret Jonas

RUDOLF STEINER PRESS

Rudolf Steiner Press
Hillside House, The Square
Forest Row, RH18 5ES

www.rudolfsteinerpress.com

Published by Rudolf Steiner Press 2009

Earlier English publications: see Sources section on p. 244

Originally published in German in various volumes of the GA (*Rudolf Steiner Gesamtausgabe* or Collected Works) by Rudolf Steiner Verlag, Dornach. For further information see Sources, p. 244. This authorized translation is published by permission of the Rudolf Steiner Nachlassverwaltung, Dornach

All material has been translated or checked against the original German by Christian von Arnim

A catalogue record for this book is available from the British Library

ISBN: 978 1 85584 223 6

Cover by Andrew Morgan Design
Typeset by DP Photosetting, Neath, West Glamorgan
Printed and bound by Gutenberg Press Limited, Malta

Mixed Sources
Product group from well-managed forests, and other controlled sources
www.fsc.org Cert no. TT-CoC-002424
© 1996 Forest Stewardship Council
FSC

The paper used for this book is FSC-certified and totally chlorine-free. FSC (the Forest Stewardship Council) is an international network to promote responsible management of the world's forests.

Contents

Introduction

How did Rudolf Steiner view the connection between astrology and astronomy? Did he perceive one at all? In one sense his whole work embraces both. There is hardly a lecture that does not relate the human being to the cosmos in some way; it is an intrinsic part of the anthroposophical world-view. As these lectures and extracts will show, we are created by cosmic beings who are connected to planets and stars, which are not perceived as dead rock or mere gas. That there is meaning in the stars is naturally difficult for the astronomer to accept without undergoing the necessary preparation of widening his or her thinking and understanding. It becomes more complex when the question of astrology is introduced. In the Middle Ages, *Astronomia* (one of the Seven Liberal Arts) was as much astrology as astronomy, whereas nowadays 'astronomy' is reserved for understanding the physical attributes of the universe—mainly size, distance, speed and so on. 'Astrology' gives meaning to the stars and planets. It can be said to be a 'soul level' of understanding, whilst beyond that a third term is sometimes used: 'astrosophy'—wisdom of the stars, a spiritual level. In fact if any of the three 'levels' is carried out with true understanding of what is really involved, the other two are present also. Astrology and astronomy parted company around the seventeenth century; though figures like Sir Isaac Newton continued to look at horoscopes, the notion of stars and planets being connected to human destiny disappeared for astronomers who were holding to an increasingly materialistic world-view, which left no room for spiritual or soul qualities manifesting in the natural world. Astronomers may reject astrology as superstition, but what do they offer in its place? Speculation becomes dogma and they look for explanations rather than meaning. Concepts such as 'millions of galaxies', 'light years', 'black holes', 'red dwarfs' render the vast interstellar spaces so infinitely empty that we may be filled with a cold terror. Following space probes on radio telescopes or tracking planets on computer programs becomes an intellectual abstraction which equally separates us from *meaning* in the universe, whilst giving the illusion of understanding to the one staring at a screen from the comfort of home or workplace. 'Naked-eye astronomy' can be one attempt to redress the abstraction, but may still leave us without meaning.

We can see that Rudolf Steiner struggled with the question of astrology. On the one hand he makes clear that there is a connection between stars and human beings, but on the other he appears uncomfortable with what is generally thought of as astrology, and certainly he rejects the notion of stars and planets determining our lives and behaviour. This rejection is not as simplistic as might be supposed, for freedom lies in our thoughts not in our will: 'Read my *Philosophy of Spiritual Activity*[1] and see how much importance I attach to the point that one should not ask about the freedom of the will. The will lies deep, deep down in the unconscious, and it is nonsense to ask about the freedom of the will. It is only of the freedom of thoughts that we can speak... Man must become free in his thoughts, and the free thoughts must give the impulse to the will—then he is free.'[2]

It is in our will that our karmic intentions are stored, intentions which have been prepared during the long period spent between lifetimes in the company of spiritual beings of the planetary spheres and beyond. But can these intentions be read in a horoscope? Whilst criticizing the superficial nature of much astrology, Steiner shows that we do indeed attempt to choose an appropriate birth time to match the destiny which we are to live out. The ability to make use of this will depend on the level of development of the astrologer concerned. (The whole question of 'unnatural' births', e.g. induced or by Caesarean section, or indeed *in vitro* fertilization is too complex to be discussed here.) The opening essay from 1905 makes clear how Steiner regarded the necessary 'qualifications' for this interpreting, how ideally the level of *Intuition*—that of being able to become one with the object perceived in order to receive its meaning—must be reached. On occasions he himself made use of horoscopes as we can see in the case of the 'special needs' children.

It can be argued that astrology has come a long way since Steiner's lifetime, less and less is the view a deterministic one. Many astrologers today embrace a spiritual world-view that often includes reincarnation and karma. Most certainly they look at the soul characteristics, which they interpret from a horoscope, and realize that everything depends on what the individual has made of the starry inheritance. They no longer speak in absolute terms of good fortune or great danger but recognize that each individual will have a unique relationship to a pattern that may be identical for dozens of people. With this view it can be a valuable tool in therapy or counselling. It should be evident that popular 'sun sign' columns in papers or on websites are not what are meant here. That people are gullible over horoscopes has been demonstrated by the French researcher Michel Gauquelin who gave identical interpretations of what was in fact the horoscope of a notorious murderer to a number of satisfied clients! Further examples have been demonstrated on television programmes of people receiving the same interpretation worded in a very generic way and being delighted that it describes them so well. This sort of general interpretation and uncritical appraisal is probably more what Steiner had in mind to criticize. But even with the more serious astrologers he would ask: why should it be that this is so? From where or what does your information derive? In short, tradition is not enough. The astrologer today would be required to understand the human and cosmic connections as deeply as possible.

Steiner was also critical of what he felt was unduly egotistic in wanting to know one's destiny from a horoscope. This may be the case for someone who is told that he or she has such and such fine qualities or abilities, but it can also be the case that we can learn more about our weaknesses and difficulties from the birth chart, though, as he pointed out to Elisabeth Vreede, this does not mean we should try to avoid challenging periods.[3] We should avoid being tempted to 'fear' the planets. It is said that one of his many lectures was planned for a day when planetary aspects were considered very 'bad' and local organizers suggested changing it, which he firmly refused to do, with apparently no serious consequences! He was not, however, averse to choosing a propitious time for an event when it meant that a deed performed in some way echoed or, rather, spoke back to the cosmos in the sense of the verse quoted at the end of the selection (p. 236). This is shown by the time chosen for the powerful ceremony of the laying of the foundation stone of the first Goetheanum in Dornach in 1913. He placed a document with the stone, which included the wording that Mercury as evening star was setting in the sign of Libra: '... for the work of anthroposophy on the 20th day of September 1880 after the Mystery of Golgotha, that is

1913 after the birth of Christ when Mercury as the evening
star stood in Libra . . .'[4] His co-worker Elisabeth Vreede, who
became the first leader of the Section for Astronomy and
Mathematics, has written about the significance of this.[5]

The simple statement that Mercury stood in Libra brings
us to another consideration that complicates the practice and
understanding of both astrology and astronomy and is one
reason why the adherents of the latter often reject the former.
An astronomical explanation is needed here. The zodiac
comprises those constellations against which the planets are
seen to move; it is also called the ecliptic, and is found to be
at an angle to the earth's equator. Moreover the earth wob-
bles slightly on its axis, a movement called nutation. This
results in the phenomenon known as the precession of the
equinoxes, meaning that if one takes the spring equinox to
coincide with the first degree of Aries, as most astrologers do,
then the starry backdrop is no longer seen to coincide. At the
time of Christ they did coincide, but before and after different constellations could be seen, which are taken to mark
great cultural ages (see extract no. 19). Thus today the
remaining stars of the constellation of Pisces can be seen
here, and within a century or two those of Aquarius will rise.
Most western astrologers—in the East it is different, Indian
astrology (*jyotish*) uses the sidereal, i.e. the starry constellations for horoscopes—with some exceptions use the so-called
'tropical', meaning that it takes its basis from the beginning
of Aries at the spring equinox. It would take too long in this
introduction to discuss the reasons for this or the pros and
cons. One justification for using the tropical zodiac, quite
apart from tradition, comes from a statement by Johannes
Kepler who was court astrologer to the Duke of Wallenstein,
casting horoscopes as well as peering through the newly

invented telescope at the moons of Jupiter. He still understood the earth as an ensouled being and had a feeling for the difference the coming of Christ made to the earth, writing that: 'A certain image of the zodiac and of the whole firmament is imprinted by God in the soul of the earth.'[6]

Heinz Walther describes this further as follows: 'The aura of the earth has absorbed into herself the image of the zodiac. The earth now bears firmly its image, the earth to which the beneficent gods by that decisive event gave a new direction into the sense of the world plan. The sun ... defines by its annual course the division of the zodiac as it is decisive for us today...'[7] In other words, with the coming of Christ to the earth its etheric aura was penetrated by the Christ Being from the sun to allow an imprint from the constellations to occur. There is plenty of evidence of the suitability of the tropical zodiac for understanding a human being's earthly path and destiny. More spiritual considerations however may be revealed by the actual constellations. The use of these has been found to work better for the biodynamic method of farming and gardening, though differing research results have been produced by the fact of differing opinions as to the constellations' actual boundaries. See the work of Maria Thun in her annual sowing and planting calendar.[8] Her insights are based on Lili Kolisko's pioneering experiments studying the effect of planetary movements on metal solutions.[9] Nick Kollerstrom, by contrast, uses different boundaries in his annual calendar, based on Robert Powell's research into the sidereal zodiac.[10] It may surprise some people that the *Mercury in Libra* event refers not to the actual constellation but to the 'tropical sign'. Thus for earthly deeds Kepler's words can be shown to have some significance, for Steiner's comments on these followed not long after the laying of the foundation stone event. Nevertheless this question of 'which zodiac' is unresolved both within anthroposophical circles and outside. Another unresolved question is what happens in the more northerly (or southerly) latitudes beyond 67°. Certain signs do not rise or set and a normal horoscope cannot be cast. Yet considerable numbers of people live in these regions—Scandinavia, Canada and Siberia for example. This points to the need for much further understanding of how the mystery of birth and earthly destiny descends from out of the planetary spheres, which has hardly begun.

People in earlier civilizations possessed more in the way of a visionary capacity and related to the stars in different ways. In northern and western Europe the emphasis was more on trying to understand the nature of the sun's passage through the constellations by means of erecting stone circles, cromlechs and small chambers and perceiving the quality of the shadows cast as well as the sun's movement at the solstice points. Eclipses—often feared in those times—could also be foretold by the positions and orientations of the stars. The work of Professor Alexander Thom and others have revealed these remarkable observatories.[11] Further south, priests and priestesses also gave practical indications from observing the heavens but the emphasis was more on the path of the human soul and its destiny, such as with the peoples of Egypt and Babylonia with their pyramids and seven-tiered ziggurats. With the Chinese and other more northerly peoples the circumpolar stars were at least as important as the zodiac. *Arthur—The Great Bear, Odin's Wagon, The Golden Dagger or Plough of Jamshyd*—such names are a reminder of the myths deriving from this earlier visionary state. Today we have reincarnated people from many of these ancient mysteries, so it is hardly surprising that approaches can be so different. During Roman times astrology became more decadent partly due to the attitude of figures such as the Emperor Tiberius who had his astrologers put to death if they dared to say something that displeased him. The birth of the earthly vehicle for Christ was foretold by a star as we are told by St Matthew and wise men from the region of Iran understood its meaning. As much as they read the meaning of the starry script, they also saw clairvoyantly the descent of the soul of their teacher Zarathustra (Zoroaster = Golden Star) who was reincarnating on earth to prepare the vessel of the Christ.[12]

With the spread of Arabic science in Europe, ancient astrological texts came to be translated and circulated. However the notion of a fixed fate also arose—*It is written*—which is hard to detach from astrology today and which led inevitably to the rejection of it as mere superstition as people discovered a greater freedom in their own thinking and a greater autonomy in their life paths. Rudolf Steiner aimed to show that it is not necessary to reject any connection with the stars and planets in order to be a fully modern person, and indeed the pursuit of it with the right understanding gives a far greater meaning to our earthly lives. Moreover the spiritual beings are waiting to hear from human beings on earth, for remarkable as it may sound we are the religion of the gods: 'Thus the gods have the image of the human being before them as their highest ideal, their religion.'[13] It is in this spirit that one may presume to attempt an understanding of how astrology relates to this ideal human being.

'We will then realize that while people looked to the constellations of the stars in ancient times to understand human destiny on earth, we must now look to the human being, permeated by the Christ substance here on earth while possessing full humanness, who then lights up for the universe. The human being lights up as the star of humanity after having gone through the portal of death.'[14]

Isis-Sophia, the heavenly wisdom perceived by ancient peoples as arrayed in a cloak decorated with stars, can be our guide on this journey. In conclusion may we also remember, as the final extract shows, that our connection to the heavenly bodies is maintained by the grace of the Archangel Michael, the Spirit of our age.

* * *

Extracts of a more purely astronomical nature have not been included as this compilation is not intended for the specialist and they would require much explanation, but suggestions for further reading are to be found at the end. Other important omissions are the many lectures on the connections between spiritual hierarchies and the planets because this is a lengthy study in its own right. Also omitted is the correlation of philosophical world-views and the zodiac for the same reason, and likewise other specialized material such as eurythmy gestures, planets and zodiac. Steiner's legacy in this whole area was carried on most worthily by Elisabeth Vreede, whose astronomical letters[15] cannot be recommended enough for providing elucidation of many of Steiner's statements. Other researchers such as Willi Sucher and Robert Powell have made valuable contributions even if methods and views differ. There is a growing body of work in the United States and in Germany also, originally pioneered by Guenther Wachsmuth and Werner Böhm.

Margaret Jonas

1. How does theosophy regard astrology?

In this early essay of 1905, written for the theosophical journal Luzifer-Gnosis, *which Rudolf Steiner also edited, he sets the scene for the whole later development of his cosmology within anthroposophy. He also states the necessity of realizing that one can only really practise astrology if one takes into account successive earth lives, and moreover works upon oneself in order to reach the level of development he called Intuition—meaning not the rather vague sense for the significance of something coming to a person, which is ordinarily meant, but the capacity to be able to so unite with a percept or being that its true nature is revealed to one.*

Another question was asked: 'How does theosophy relate to astrology?'
To begin with, it has to be said in this context that very little is known currently as to what astrology really is. Because what is often presented as such in handbooks is a purely outer compilation of rules the deeper meaning of which is hardly ever explained. Methods of calculation are specified by means of which certain constellations of the stars at the time of a person's birth or for the timing of some other important event can be determined. Then people say that such constellations have this or that meaning without any indication being given as to why it might be so or, indeed, merely how it might be so. It is therefore not surprising that people in our age consider all these things to be nonsense, bogus and superstition. Because the whole thing appears to be based on quite arbitrary assertions, made up out of thin air. At best,

people say that everything in the world is probably connected and that therefore the constellation of the sun, Venus and moon at the birth of a person might very well have an effect on his or her life, and suchlike. But true astrology is a wholly intuitive science and requires the development of higher supersensory powers of perception in those who wish to practise it, and these powers *can* only be present in a minimum number of people today. And even if we just wish to explain its basic character this requires dealing with the highest cosmological problems as set out in spiritual science. That is why only a few very general points can be made here.

The system of the stars, to which we human beings belong, is a whole. And human beings are connected with all the forces in this system of stars. Only gross materialism would believe that the human being is connected with the earth alone. We only need to look at the relationship between the human being, the sun and the moon as set out in the Akasha Chronicle.[16] It will be seen from this that there was a stage of human development in primeval times in which human beings lived on a celestial body which still consisted of the sun, moon and earth together. That is why human beings today still have forces in their nature which are related to those of these celestial bodies. These relationships still today govern a link between the effects of these celestial bodies and what happens in the human being. However, these effects are very different from the effects of a purely material nature to which alone science today refers. The sun, for example, affects human beings through something which is quite different from what science calls gravity, light and heat. Equally, there are relationships of a supersensory nature between Mars, Mercury and the other planets and human beings. On that basis, anyone who has the disposition can gain an idea of a web of supersensory connections between the celestial bodies and the beings who inhabit them. But raising such connections to the level of clear, scientific understanding requires the development of the forces of a very high level of supersensory vision. Only the highest degrees of intuition which human beings can reach are sufficient. Not the kind of blurred and semi-visionary dreaming which is now so frequently called intuition, but the most pronounced inner capacity of the senses which can only be compared to mathematical thinking.

Now there were, and still are, people in the esoteric schools who can pursue astrology in this sense. And what is written in the accessible books on this subject did in some way and at some time come from such esoteric teachers. The only thing is that anything connected with these things is inaccessible to conventional thinking, even when it is written in books, because understanding them itself requires profound intuition. And what was then transcribed of the real matters that these teachers taught by those who themselves did not understand such matters will hardly, of course, give people trapped in the current way of thinking a favourable impression of astrology. But it must nevertheless be said that even such books are not altogether worthless. Because the less people understand what they are transcribing, the better the transcription they make. They do not spoil it through their own wisdom. That is why astrological writings, no matter how obscure their origins, always contains pearls of truth for those who are capable of Intuition—but only for those. In general, astrological writings are, of their kind, better even than those of many other branches of knowledge.

In this context there is a comment which should not be omitted. There is currently the greatest confusion about the term Intuition. It must be clearly understood that science today, if it is familiar with the concept of Intuition at all, is only so in the field of mathematics. Among all our sciences this is the only field of knowledge based on pure inner perception. But such inner perception does not exist just with regard to spatial dimensions and figures but also with regard to all other things. Goethe,[17] for example, attempted to establish such an intuitive science in the field of botany. His 'archetypal plant' in its various stages of metamorphosis is based on inner perception. Reason enough for current science to have no idea of the importance of Goethe in this respect. For many higher fields, theosophy provides knowledge through inner perception. Its observations about reincarnation and karma are based on it. It should come as no surprise that people who have no idea of what is important in Goethe are also totally incapable of understanding the sources of theosophical teaching. Precisely the deeper study of valuable writings such as Goethe's *Metamorphosis of Plants* could be excellent preparation for theosophy. Of course many theosophists, too, lack patience in this respect. But once one has worked one's way through to an understanding of what is important by means of such an intuitive work as we have just mentioned, full of life as it is, one will find where the path leads. Nevertheless, the laws of astrology in turn are based on intuitions of a kind in comparison to which the knowledge of reincarnation and karma is still very elementary.

These observations are undeniably hardly comprehensive, but they might nevertheless give a vague idea about a matter of which most of those who fight it have no knowledge and of which many of those who defend it have rather skewed ideas. But what you should not do, is take an understanding of these things as an impractical activity without value and without any bearing on real, practical life. When they find their way into the supersensory worlds, human beings grow not just in terms of their knowledge but above all in moral terms and in their soul. Even a vague idea of their position in the context of the stellar system acts on their individual character, on their actions and the direction they give to the whole of their existence. And to a much greater extent than many people today imagine, the progress of our social life depends on the progress of human beings on the path to supersensory knowledge. Anyone with some insight knows that our current social situation is only an expression of the materialism which underlies our knowledge. And once such a kind of knowledge is replaced by a spiritual one, then the outer conditions of our life will also improve.

2. Prophecy: its nature and meaning

This long out of print public lecture has been included because it deals considerably with the nature of foretelling the future—one traditional role of astrology now partly superseded in the West by a more 'counselling' approach. It is remarkable that Kepler's horoscope for Wallenstein[18] was a 'blind' reading. As with ancient peoples, a more psychic faculty was perhaps also working in Kepler. Steiner goes on to encourage us to look at the rhythms in our lives—working with events that happened at particular ages— and from there, the importance of seven-year life periods. He makes clear that one does not look to the stars as causes of events but to indicate the timing—*a cosmic clock in fact. That this timing is incorporated into our etheric body at conception is shown in a later extract. The respect for seership performed in tranquillity with devotion is also evident.*

Words spoken by Shakespeare's most famous character, 'There are more things in heaven and earth than are dreamed of in your philosophy,'[19] are, of course, perfectly true. But no less true is the saying composed by Lichtenberg, a great German humorist, as a kind of rejoinder: 'In philosophy there is much that will be found neither in heaven nor earth.' Both sayings are illustrations of the attitude adopted nowadays to many things in the domain of spiritual science. It seems inevitable that widespread circles, especially in the world of serious science, will repudiate such matters as prophecy even more emphatically than other branches of spiritual science. If in these other branches of spiritual science—in many of them at least—it is difficult to draw a clear line between genuine research and charlatanism, or maybe something even worse, it will certainly be admitted that wherever supersensible investigation touches the element of human egoism, there its dangers begin. And in what realm of higher knowledge could this be more apparent than in all that is comprised in the theme of prophecy as it has appeared through the ages! Everything covered by the term 'prophecy' is closely connected with a widespread—and understandable—trait in the human mind, namely, desire to penetrate the darkness of the future, to know something of what earthly life in the future holds in store.

Interest in prophecy is connected not only with curiosity in the ordinary sense but with curiosity concerning very intimate regions of the human soul. The search for knowledge concerning the deeper interests of the human soul has met with so many disappointments that earnest, serious science nowadays is unwilling to listen to such matters—and this is really not to be wondered at. Nevertheless it looks as though our times will be obliged at least to take notice of them, and also of the subjects of which we have been speaking in previous lectures and shall speak in the future. As will be known to many of you, the historian Kemmerich has written a book about prophecies, his aim being to compile facts that can be confirmed by history and go to show that important happenings were precognized or predicted in some way. This historian is driven to make the statement—at the moment we will not question the authenticity of his research—that there are very few important events in history which have not at some time been predicted, conjectured and announced in advance. Such statements are not well received in our time; but ultimately, in the sphere where history can speak with authority, it will not be possible to ignore them because proof will be forthcoming, both in respect of the past and of the present, from outer documents themselves.

The domain we are considering today has never been in such disrepute as it is nowadays, nor regarded as so dubious a path of human endeavour. Only a few centuries ago, for instance in the sixteenth century, very distinguished and influential scholars engaged in prognostication and prophecy. Think of one of the greatest natural scientists of all time and of his connection with a personage whose tendency to be influenced by prophecies is well known: think of Kepler, the great scientist, and his relations with Wallenstein. Schiller's deep interest in this latter personality was due in no small measure to the part played in his life by prophecy. The kind of prophecy in vogue in the days of Kepler—and only a couple of centuries ago leading scientific minds all over Europe were still occupied with it—was based upon the then prevailing view that there is a real connection between the world of the stars, the movements and positions of the stars, and the life of the human being. All prophesying in those times was really a form of astrology. The mere mention of this word reminds us that in our day, too, many people are still convinced that there is some connection between the stars and coming events in the life of individuals, and even of races. But prophetic knowledge, the prophetic art as it is called, was never so directly connected with observation of the movements and constellations of the stars as was the case in Kepler's time.

In ancient Greece an art of prophecy was practised, as you know, by prophetesses or seeresses. It was an art of predicting the future induced by experiences arising perhaps from asceticism or other experiences leading to the suppression of full self-consciousness and the presence of mind of ordinary life. The human being was thus given over to other powers, was in an ecstatic condition and then made utterances which were either direct predictions of the future or were interpreted by the listening priests and soothsayers as referring to the future. We need only think of the Pythia at Delphi who under the influence of vapours rising from a chasm in the earth was transported into a state of consciousness quite different from that of ordinary life; she was controlled by other powers and in this condition made prophetic utterances. This kind of prophecy has nothing to do with calculations of the movements of stars, constellations and the like. Again, everyone is familiar with the gift of prophecy among the people of the Old Testament, the authenticity of which will certainly be called into question by modern scholarship. Out of the mouths of these prophets there came not only utterances of deep wisdom which influenced the life of these Old Testament people, but foreshadowed the future. These predictions, however, were by no means always based upon the heavenly constellations as in the astrology current in the fifteenth and sixteenth centuries. Either as the result of inborn gifts or ascetic practices and the like, these prophets unfolded a different kind of consciousness from that of the people around them; they were torn away from the affairs of ordinary life. In such a condition they were entirely detached from the circumstances and thoughts of their personal lives, from their own material environment. Their attention was focused entirely on their people, on the weal and woe of their people. Because they experienced something superhuman, something reaching beyond the individual concerns of human beings, they broke through the boundaries of their personal consciousness and it was as though Yahweh himself spoke out of their mouths, so wise were their utterances concerning the tasks and the destiny of their people.

Thinking of all this, it seems evident that the kind of divination practised at the end of the Middle Ages, before the dawn of modern science, was only one specific form and that prophecy as a whole is a much wider sphere, connected in some way with definite states of consciousness which a human being can only attain when he throws off the shackles of his personality. Astrological prophecy, of course, can hardly be said to be an art in which a human being rises above his own personality. The astrologer is given the date and hour of birth and from this discovers which constellation was rising on the horizon and the relative positions of other stars and constellations. From this he calculates how the positions of the constellations will change during the course of the person's life and, according to certain traditional observations of the favourable or unfavourable influences of heavenly bodies upon human life, predicts from these calculations what will transpire in the life of an individual or of a people. There seems to be no kind of similarity between this type of astrologer and the ancient Hebrew prophets, the Greek seeresses or others who, having passed out of their ordinary consciousness into a state of ecstasy, foretold the future entirely from knowledge acquired in the realm of the supersensible. For those who consider themselves enlightened, educated people today, the greatest stumbling block in these astrological predictions is the difficulty in understanding how the courses of the stars and constellations can possibly have any connection with happenings in the life of an individual or a people, or in the procession of events on the earth. And as the attention of modern scholarship is never focused on such connections no particular interest is taken in what was accepted as authentic knowledge in times when astrological prophecy and enlightened science often went hand in hand.

Kepler, the very distinguished and learned scientist, was not only the discoverer of the laws named after him; not only was he one of the greatest astronomers of all time, but he devoted himself to astrological prophecy. In his time—also during the periods immediately preceding and following it— numbers of truly enlightened men were votaries of this art. Indeed if we think objectively about life as it was in those days, we realize that from their standpoint it was as natural to them to take this prophetic art, this prophetic knowledge, as seriously as our contemporaries take any genuine branch of science. When some prediction based upon the constellations and made, perhaps, at the birth of an individual comes true later on, it is of course easy to say that the connection of this constellation with the person's life was only a matter of chance. Certainly it must be admitted in countless cases that astonishment at the fulfilment of astrological prediction is caused simply because it came true and because people have forgotten what did not come true. The contention of a certain Greek atheist is, in a sense, correct. He once came in his ship to a coastal town where, in a sanctuary, tokens had been hung by people who had vowed at sea that if they were saved from shipwreck they would make such offerings. Many, many tokens were hanging there—all of them the offerings of people who had been saved from shipwreck. But the atheist maintained that the truth could only be brought to light if the tokens of everyone who, in spite of their vows, had actually perished in shipwreck were also displayed. It would then be obvious to which category the greater number of tokens belonged. This implies that a really objective judgement could only be reached if records were kept not only of those astrological predictions which have come true but also of those which have not. This attitude is perfectly justified but on the other hand there is certainly much that is very astonishing. As in these public lectures I cannot take for granted a fundamental knowledge of all the teachings of spiritual science, I must also refer to things which can convey to the general public an idea of the significance of the subjects we are studying.

Even a confirmed sceptic must surely feel surprise when he hears the following. Keeping to well-known personages, let us take the case of Wallenstein. Wallenstein wished to have his horoscope drawn up by Kepler—a name honoured by every scientist. Kepler sent the horoscope. But the matter had been arranged with caution. Wallenstein did not write to Kepler giving him the year of his birth and saying that he would like him to draw up the horoscope, but an intermediary was chosen. Kepler therefore did not know for whom the horoscope was intended. The only indication given was the date of the birth. There had already been many important happenings in Wallenstein's life and he requested that they too should be recorded, as well as predictions made of those still to come. Kepler completed the horoscope as requested. As is the case with many horoscopes, Wallenstein found very much that tallied with his experiences. He began—as happened with so many people in that time—to have great confidence in Kepler and on many occasions was able to adjust his life according to the prognostications. But it must be said, too, that although many things tallied many did not, so far as the past was concerned, and as subsequently transpired the same was true of the predictions made about the future. It was so with numbers of horoscopes and in those days people were accustomed to say that there must be some inaccuracy in the alleged hour of birth and that the astrologer might be able to correct it. Wallenstein did the same. He asked Kepler to correct the hour of birth; the correction was only very slight but after it had been made, the prognostications were more accurate. It must be added here that Kepler was a thoroughly honest man and it went very much against the grain to correct the hour of birth. From a letter on the subject written by Kepler at the time it is obvious that he did not favour such a procedure on account of the many possible consequences. Nevertheless he undertook to do what Wallenstein asked—this happened in 1625—and gave further details about Wallenstein's future; above all he said that according to the new reading of the positions of the stars, the constellation that would be present in the year 1634 would be extremely unfavourable for Wallenstein. Kepler added that, since the date lay so far ahead, even if Wallenstein became upset his upset would have passed by the time these unfavourable circumstances came to pass. He did not consider them a danger to Wallenstein's plans. The prediction was for March 1634. And now just think: a few weeks before the period indicated the causes occurred which led to the murder of Wallenstein. These things are at least striking!

But let us take other examples—not from second-rate astrologers but from really enlightened people. The name of an extraordinarily learned man in this sphere will at once occur to us—Nostradamus.[23] Nostradamus was a doctor of high repute who, among other activities, had rendered wonderful service during an epidemic of the plague; he was a man of profound gifts, and the selflessness with which he devoted himself to his profession as a doctor is well known. It is known, too, that when on account of his selflessness he had been much maligned by his colleagues, he retired from his medical work to the isolation of Salon where he died. In Salon he began to observe the stars, but not as Kepler or others like Kepler had observed them. Nostradamus had a special room in his house into which he often withdrew and, as can be gathered from what he himself says, from this room he watched the stars, just as they presented themselves to his gaze. In other words he made no special mathematical calculations but immersed himself in what the soul, the heart, the imagination can discover when gazing with wonder at the starry heavens. Nostradamus spent many an hour of reverent, fervent contemplation in this curious chamber with its open views on all sides to the heavens. And we have from him not only specific predictions but long series of diverse and remarkably true prophecies of the future. So much so, that Kemmerich, the historian of whom I spoke just now, could not but be astonished and attach a certain value to the prophetic utterances of Nostradamus a long time after they were made. Nostradamus himself made some of his prophecies known to the public and was naturally laughed to scorn in his day, for he could quote no astrological calculations. As he gazed at the stars his predictions seemed to rise up in him in the form of strange pictures and imaginations, for instance of the outcome of the battle at Gravelingen in the year 1558, where the French were defeated with heavy losses. Another prediction, made long beforehand, for the year 1559, was to the effect that King Henry II of France would succumb 'in a duel' as Nostradamus put it. People only laughed, including the Queen herself, who said that this clearly showed what reliance could be placed upon prediction—for a king was above engaging in a duel. But what happened? In the year predicted, the King was killed in a tournament. And it would be possible to quote many, many predictions which subsequently came true.

Then again there is Tycho Brahe,[20] one of the brilliant minds of the sixteenth century and of outstanding significance as an astronomer. The modern world knows little of Tycho Brahe beyond that he is said to have been one who only half accepted the Copernican view of the world. But those who are more closely acquainted with his life know what Tycho Brahe achieved in the making of celestial charts, how vastly he improved the charts then existing, that he had discovered new stars and was, in short, an astronomer of great eminence in his day. Tycho Brahe was also deeply convinced that not only are physical conditions on the earth connected with the whole universe, but that the spiritual experiences of human beings are connected with happenings in the great cosmos. Tycho Brahe did not simply observe the stars as an astronomer but he related the happenings of human life to happenings in the heavens. And when he came to Rostock at the age of 20, he caused a stir by predicting the death of the Sultan Suleiman, which, although it did not occur exactly on the day indicated, did nevertheless occur. The indication was not quite exact but the lack of precision was not so great that it would have given historians, say, cause to complain. One might well argue that if anyone were intent upon lying he would not tell a half-lie by introducing the difference of a mere day or so into the prediction.

Hearing of this, the King of Denmark requested Tycho Brahe to cast the horoscopes of his three sons. Concerning his son Christian, the indications were accurate; less so in the case of Ulrich. But about Hans, the third son, Tycho Brahe made a remarkable prediction derived from the movements of the stars. He said that the whole constellation and everything to be seen went to show that Duke Hans is and will remain frail and is unlikely to live to a great age. As the hour of birth was not quite accurate, Tycho Brahe gave the indications very cautiously: he might die in his eighteenth or perhaps in his nineteenth year, for the constellations then would be extremely unfavourable. I will leave it an open question whether it was out of pity for the parents or for other reasons that Tycho Brahe wrote of the possibility that this terrible constellation in the eighteenth or nineteenth year might be overcome in the life of Duke Hans. If it were, God would have been his protector. But it had to be realized that these conditions would be there, that an extremely unfavourable constellation connected with Mars was revealed by the horoscope and that Hans would be entangled in the complications of war; as in this constellation Venus had ascendancy over Mars, there was just a hope that Hans would pass this period safely. But then, in his eighteenth or nineteenth year, there would be the very unfavourable constellation due to the inimical influence of Saturn; this indicated the risk of a 'moist, melancholic' illness caused by the strange environment in which Hans would find himself. And now, what was the history of Duke Hans's life? As a young man he was involved in the political complications of the time, was sent to war, took part in the Battle of Ostend and in connection with this, as Tycho Brahe had predicted, had to endure the ordeal of terrible storms at sea. He came very near to death, but as the result of negotiations initiated by a friendly party for his marriage to the daughter of the Czar he was recalled to Denmark. According to Tycho Brahe's interpretation, the complications due to the unfavourable influences of Mars had been stemmed by the influences of Venus—the protector of love relationships. Venus had protected the Duke at this time. But then, in his eighteenth, nineteenth year the inimical influence of Saturn began to take effect. One can picture how the eyes of the Danish Court were upon the young Duke. All the preparations for the marriage were made and the news that it had taken place was hourly awaited. But there came instead the announcement that the marriage was delayed, then news of the Duke's illness, and finally of his death. Such things made a great impression upon people at the time and must surely also astonish posterity.

Now world history sometimes has its humorous sides! There was once, in a different domain altogether, a certain professor who asserted that the brain of the female always weighs less than that of the male. After his death, however, his own brain was weighed and proved to be extremely light. He was the victim of humour in world history!

The same happened to Pico de Mirandola whose horoscope predicted that Mars would bring him great misfortune. He was an opponent of all such predictions. Tycho Brahe proved to him that all his arguments against prognostications from the stars were false, and he died in the year that had been indicated as the period of the unfavourable influence of Mars.

Numbers of examples could be quoted and we shall probably realize that in a certain sense it is not difficult to make objections. For example, a very distinguished modern astronomer—a man greatly to be respected, too, for his humanitarian activities—has argued that Wallenstein's death cannot be said to have been correctly predicted in the horoscope drawn up by Kepler. In a certain respect such arguments must be taken seriously. We cannot altogether ignore Friedrich Wilhelm Foerster's argument that Wallen-

stein knew what had been predicted; that in the corresponding year he remembered his horoscope, hesitated, did
not take the firm stand he would otherwise have taken and so
was himself the cause of the misfortune. Such objections are
always possible.

But on the other side it must be taken into consideration
that, to the extent that evidence based on external data is of
value at all, there is absolutely sufficient information for the
modern age to posit facts which—let us say—do not require
more precise evidence. Many things may be problematical.
But we should not shut our eyes to the fact that careful
comparison of events that have actually occurred in life with
indications obtained from the stars did indeed lead, in earlier
times, to confidence in prognostications of the future. People
were certainly alive to mistakes but they did not conceal
things that were genuinely astonishing, nor did they accept
these things entirely without criticism. In those times too
they were quite capable of criticism and in all probability
applied it on many occasions.

I wanted to quote very striking examples in order to show
that in accordance with the standards of modern science, too,
it is possible to take these matters seriously. And even if we
accept the objections, if we wholly reject the content of these
matters, we shall have to admit that the reasons which in
relatively recent times made brilliant minds place reliance in
them were not bad but sound and well-founded reasons.
Even if these reasons are rejected, it must be admitted that
the impression they made on brilliant and enlightened minds
was such that these men believed—quite apart from details—
that there is a connection between events in the lives of
individuals and of peoples, and happenings in the cosmos.
These men believed that there is a real connection between

the macrocosm, the great world, and the microcosm, the little world.

They believed that human life on the earth is not a chaotic flow of events but that laws are manifest in these events, that just as celestial events are governed by cyclical laws so too certain cyclical laws, a certain rhythm is manifest in human and earthly conditions. To explain what is meant here, I shall speak of certain facts which can be the subject of experience as truly as the most exacting facts of chemistry or physics today. But the observations must be made in the appropriate spheres. Suppose we observe something that happens in a human being's life during his childhood. If we study the longer sweep of human life, remarkable connections will come to light, for example, between the life of earliest childhood and that of very old age; a connection is perceptible between what a human being experiences in the twilight of his life and what he experienced in early youth. We can say: if when we were young we experienced particular states of fear we may very well not be bothered by them throughout our life, but in old age things may appear of which we know that their causes are to be sought in very early childhood. Again there are connections between the years of adolescence and the period immediately preceding old age. Life runs a circular course.

We can go still further, taking as an example the case of someone who, say at the age of 18, was torn right away from the course his life had taken so far. Until then he may have been able to devote himself to study but was suddenly obliged to abandon this and become a businessman, perhaps because his father lost his money or for some other reason. To begin with he gets on quite well but after a few years great inner difficulties make their appearance. In trying to help such a person to overcome these difficulties, we cannot apply any general, abstract principles. We shall have to say to ourselves: at the age of 18 there was a sudden change in his life and at the age of 24—that is to say, six years later—difficulties cropped up in his inner life. Six years earlier, in his twelfth year or thereabouts, certain things happened in his soul which actually explain the difficulties appearing in his twenty-fourth year: six years before, six years later—the change of profession lies between. Just as above a pendulum swinging to right and left there is a point of equilibrium, so, in the case quoted, the eighteenth year is a pivotal point. A cause generated before this pivotal point has its effect the same number of years afterwards. So it is in the human being's life as a whole. Human life takes its course not with irregularity but with regularity and according to certain laws. Although the individual does not necessarily realize it, there is in every human life one centre-point; what lies before— youth and childhood—allows causes to rest in the depths of subsequent events, and then what took place a number of years before this centre-point of life reveals itself in its effects an equal number of years afterwards. In the sense that birth is the point polar to death, the happenings of childhood are the causes of happenings during the years which precede death. In this way life becomes comprehensible.

In the case, for example, of illness occurring, say, at the age of 54, the only really intelligent approach is to look for a pivotal point at which a person passed through a definite crisis, calculating back from there to some event related to the fifty-fourth year somewhat in the same sense as death is related to birth, or the other way round. The fact that happenings in human life conform to certain laws and principles does not contradict our freedom. One of the greatest concerns of people is usually that such conformity to certain laws in the course taken by events contradicts a person's freedom of will. But this is not the case and it can only appear so to superficial thinking. A human being who at the age, say, of 15 lays into the womb of time some cause the effects of which he experienced in, say, his fifty-fourth year no more deprives himself of his freedom than does someone who builds a house and then moves into it when it is ultimately ready. Logical thinking will never say that the person deprives himself of his freedom when he moves into the house. Nobody deprives himself of freedom by anticipating that causes will have their effects later on. This principle has nothing directly to do with freedom in life.

Just as there are cyclical connections in the life of the individual, so too there are cyclical connections in the life of peoples and in life on earth in a general sense. The evolution of humankind on earth divides itself into successive cultural epochs. Two of the epochs most closely connected with our own are the period of Assyrian-Egyptian-Chaldean civilization and that of the later culture of Greece and Rome; then, calculated from the decline of Greek and Roman culture and its aftermath, comes our present epoch. According to all the signs of the times this will last for a very long time yet. We thus have three consecutive periods of culture.

Close observation of the life of peoples during these three epochs reveals something like a pivotal point in the evolution of humankind during the Graeco-Latin period. Hence, too, the curious fascination of the culture of Greece and Rome. Greek art, Greek and Roman political life, Roman law and statecraft, the idea of Roman citizenship—it all stands like a kind of pivotal point in the stream of the human development. After it we have our own cultural epoch; before it the

Egypto-Chaldean period. In a remarkable way, those who observe deeply enough will perceive certain conditions of life during the Egypto-Chaldean period operating again today in quite a different but nevertheless related form. In those times, therefore, causes were laid into the womb of the ages which now, in their effects, come again to the fore. Certain methods of hygiene, certain ablutions customary in ancient Egypt, also certain views of life are now, strangely enough, in the forefront again—naturally in absolutely different forms. In short, the effects of causes laid down in ancient Egypt are becoming perceptible today. In between—like a fulcrum—lies the culture of Greece and Rome.

The Egypto-Chaldean epoch was preceded by that of ancient Persian culture. According to the law of cyclical evolution, then, it can be foreshadowed that just as in our civilization there is a cyclical re-emergence of Egypto-Chaldean culture, so ancient Persian culture will re-emerge in the epoch following our own. Laws operate everywhere in the flow of human evolution! Not irregularity, not chaos, but also not the kind of laws conjectured by historians: that the causes of everything happening today are to be sought in the immediately preceding period, the causes of events in the recent past again in the immediately preceding period, and so forth. This is how a chain of events is built up, the one directly following the other. Closer observation, however, reveals no such thing but the existence of cycles, overlaps, so that something that was once present remains hidden for a time and appears again at a later time, and so on. External observation of human development alone can discern this.

But it will be quite apparent to those who were present at the last two lectures and who study the evolution of humanity in the light of spiritual science that there is evidence of spiritual laws in the flow of events, in the stream of the becoming, and that when a certain deepening of the life of soul is achieved human beings may actually perceive the threads of these inner connections. And although it is not easy to grasp everything that belongs to this sphere, although it may sometimes tend to charlatanry or humbug and direct its appeal to the lower impulses and instincts, nevertheless the following is true. When a person is able to eliminate personal interests and quicken the hidden forces of spiritual life, so that his knowledge is drawn not merely from his environment or from remembrances of his own life and that of his nearest acquaintances, when he is uninfluenced by material and personal considerations, then he grows beyond his own personality and becomes conscious of the presence of higher forces, which it is only a matter of developing by appropriate exercises. When these deeper forces are brought to the surface, events in the life of a human being will also reveal their hidden causes and such a soul will then glimpse the truth that whatever has transpired through the ages throws its effects into the future. The law presented to us by spiritual science is that no events—and this also applies to the domain of the spiritual—float meaninglessly along the stream of existence; they all have their effects and we must discover the law underlying the manifestation of these effects in later times. In this way we are also able to realize in the first place that this life between birth and death also contains the causes for the return of the individuality to earth so that the causes of the effects in a next life have their causes in the present one.

Just as knowledge of the workings of karma arises from insight into how causes lie in the womb of time and appear again in transformation, so too this insight was present in all those who have taken prophecy seriously or have actually

engaged in it; they have been convinced that laws prevail in
the course taken by human life and that the soul can awaken
the forces whereby these laws may be penetrated. But the
soul needs points of focus. The world is in fact an inter-
connected whole. Just as in his physical life the human being
is affected by wind and weather, it is not difficult to assume
that there are connections in everything around us, even
though the details are obscure. Without actually seeking for
laws of nature in this context as we have them today, something in the courses of the stars and constellations evokes the
thought: the harmonies perceptible there can call forth in us
similar harmonies and rhythms according to which human
life runs its course.

Further observations will then lead on to the details. As
may be read in the little book, *Education of the Child*,[21] epochs
can be distinguished in the life of the individual: from birth to
the change of teeth, from then to puberty, then the years up
to 21 and again from 21 to 28, i.e. seven-year periods clearly
different in character and after which new kinds of faculties
are present. If we know how to investigate these things we
shall find clear evidence of a rhythmic stream in human life
which can be found again in the starry heavens. Strikingly
enough, if life is observed from this point of view—but such
observation must be calm and balanced, without the fanati-
cism of the opposition—it will be found that round about the
twenty-eighth year something in the life of soul indicates, in
many cases, a culmination of what has come into being after
four periods of seven years each. Four times seven years, 28
years, although the figure is not absolutely exact this is the
approximate time of one revolution of Saturn. Saturn
revolves in a circle consisting of four parts, passes through the
whole zodiacal circle, and its course has an actual corre-

spondence with the course of the human being's life from birth to the twenty-eighth year. Just as the circle divides into four parts, so too these 28 years divide into four periods of seven years each. There, in the revolution of a planet in cosmic space, we see indications of similarity with the course taken by human life.

Other movements in the heavens, too, correspond to rhythms in human life. Little attention is paid today to the very brilliant research of Fliess,[22] a doctor in Berlin; it is still only in the initial stages but as it is developed the rhythmic flow of births and deaths in the life of humanity will be clearly perceived. All such research is only at the beginning; but in time to come it will be realized that one need only regard the stars and their movements as a great celestial clock and human life as a rhythm which runs its own course but is in a certain sense determined by the stars. Without looking for actual causes in the stars, it is quite possible to conceive that because of this inner relationship, human life runs its course with a similar rhythm. Suppose, for example, we often go outside the door of our house or look out of the window at some particular time in the morning and always see a certain man on the way to his office, we glance at the clock, knowing that every day he will pass at a definite time. Are the hands of the clock the cause of it? Of course not! But because of the invariable rhythm we can assume that the man will pass the house at a definite time. In this sense we can see in the stars a celestial clock according to which the life of human beings and peoples runs its course.

Such things may well be vantage points for the observation and study of life, and spiritual science is able to indicate these deeper connections. We shall now understand why Tycho Brahe, Kepler and others worked on the basis of calculations—Kepler especially, Tycho Brahe less. For insight into the soul of Tycho Brahe reveals a certain similarity with that of Nostradamus.[23] Nostradamus, however, does not need to make calculations at all; he sits up in his attic and gives himself up to the impressions made by the stars. He ascribes this gift to certain inherited qualities in his organism which for this reason is no obstacle for him. But he also needs that inner tranquillity of soul which arises after he has put away all thoughts, emotions, cares, and excitements of everyday life. The soul must face the stars in purity and freedom. And then what Nostradamus prophesies rises up in him in pictures and images; he sees it all before him in pictures. If he spoke in astronomical terms of Saturn or Mars being injurious, he would not, in predicting destiny, have been thinking of the physical Saturn or the physical Mars, but he would have pondered in this way: such and such a man has a warlike nature, a temperament that loves fighting, but he also has a kind of melancholy making him subject to moods of depression which may even affect him physically. Nostradamus lets this interweave in his contemplation and a picture rises before him of future happenings in the man's life: the tendency to melancholy and the fighting spirit intermingle—Saturn and Mars. This is only a symbol. When he speaks of Saturn and Mars his meaning is: there is something in this man which presents itself to me as a picture but which can be compared with the opposition or conjunction between Saturn and Mars in the heavens. This was merely a way of expressing it; contemplation of the stars evoked in Nostradamus the seership which enabled him to see more deeply into souls than is otherwise possible.

Nostradamus, therefore, was a man who by acting in a certain way was able to waken to life inner powers of soul otherwise slumbering within the human being. In a mood of devotion, of reverence, he completely put away all cares and anxieties, all concerns of the outer world. In utter forgetfulness of self, with no feeling of his own personality, his soul knew the truth of the axiom he always quoted: it is God who speaks through my mouth. If anything I am able to tell touches on your concerns, take it as spoken to you by the grace of your God. Without such reverence there is no genuine seership. But this very attitude ensures that those who have it will not abuse or make illicit use of their gift.

Tycho Brahe represents a stage of transition between Nostradamus and Kepler. When we contemplate the soul of Tycho Brahe, he seems to be one who is calling up remembrances from an earlier life, rather reminiscent of Greek soothsaying. He has in him something that is akin to the soul of an ancient Greek seeking everywhere for the manifestations of cosmic harmony. Such is the attunement of his soul. And his astrological insight is really an attitude of soul as if astronomical calculation were merely a prop helping him to call up those powers which enable pictures of happenings in the past or the future to take shape before him. Kepler's mind is more abstract, in the sense that modern thought is abstract to a still higher degree. Kepler has to rely more or less on pure calculation in which there is, of course, accuracy, for according to knowledge derived from clairvoyance there is an actual relation between the constellations and the actions of human beings. As time went on, astrology became more and more a matter of reckoning and calculation only. The gift of seership gave place to purely intellectual thought and it can truly be said that astrological forecasts now are nothing but intellectual deduction.

The farther we go back into the past, the more we shall find that the utterances of the ancient prophets concerning the life of their peoples rose up from the very depths of their souls. So it was among the Hebrew prophets; in communion with their God and free of their personal interests and affairs, they were wholly given up to the great concerns of their people and could perceive what was in store. Just as a teacher foresees that certain qualities in a child will express themselves later on, and takes account of them, the Hebrew prophet beheld the soul of his people as one unit; the past mellowed in his soul and worked in such a way that the consequences were revealed to him as a great vision of the future.

But now, what does prophecy mean in human life, what does it really signify? We shall find the answer by thinking of the following. There are certain great figures to whom we always trace streams of events in history. Although today the preference is for everyone to be at one level because it goes against the grain when a single personality towers over all the others—in their desire that all faculties shall be equal, people are loath to admit that certain people are more forceful than the rest—in spite of this, great and advanced leaders are at work in the process of historical evolution. Things have come to such a pass nowadays that the mightiest events are conceived to be the outcome simply of ideas and not to lead back to any one personality. There is a certain school of theology which still claims to be Christian, although it contends that there need have been no Christ Jesus as an individual. In reply to the point that world history is, after all, made by people, one of these theologians said: that is as obvious as the fact that a forest is composed of trees; human beings make history in the same sense that trees make a forest. But think of it—surely the whole forest could have grown up from a few grains of seed? Certainly the forest is composed of trees but the primary step is to find out whether it did not originate from grains of seeds once laid in the soil. So, too, it is a matter of enquiring whether it is not, after all, the case that events in human evolution lead back to this or that individual who inspired the rest.

This conception of world history leads to the thought of surplus forces in those human beings who play leading parts in the evolution of humanity. Whether they apply these forces for good or ill is another matter. Human beings work upon their environment out of the surplus forces within them. Surplus forces which need not be used for personal life may express themselves in deeds or they may not find any outlet in deeds. In people of action we see how the forces in them come to direct expression in deeds. But there are others who do not have the disposition to transform their forces into deeds or, if they want to take action, some kind of obstacle always occurs. Nostradamus is an interesting example: he was a doctor, a Jew, and in this capacity brought blessing to very many people. But people often cannot stand the thought that someone is doing good. Nostradamus became an object of envy and jealousy and was accused of being a Calvinist. To be a Jew or a Calvinist was looked upon askance and circumstances therefore forced him to withdraw from his work of healing and abandon his profession. But were the forces used in this inspiring work no longer within him when he had retired? Of course they were! Physics believes in the conservation of energy or force. What happened in the case of Nostradamus was that when he gave up his work the forces in him took a different direction. If his medical activities had continued, these forces would have produced quite other effects in the future. For where can our deeds really be said to end? If, like Nostradamus, we withdraw from some activity, the flow of our deeds is suddenly stemmed—but the forces themselves are still there. The forces in Nostradamus' soul remained and were transformed—so that what might have expressed itself in deeds at some future time, rose up before him in pictures. In his case, deeds were transformed into the gift of seership. The same may be true of human beings endowed with a faculty for prophecy today; and it was true in the case of the ancient Hebrew prophets. As biblical history indicates, these men had a real connection with forces belonging to the past and to the future of their people; their own soul, their personal life, was nothing to them. They were not warlike by nature but had within them surplus forces which from the very beginning took the same form as those of Nostradamus after their transformation. Forces which in others poured into deeds revealed themselves to the Hebrew prophets in the form of mighty pictures and visions. The gift of seership is directly connected with the urge to action in human beings, with the transformation of surplus forces in the soul.

Seership is therefore by no means an incomprehensible faculty; it can be reconciled with the kind of thinking pursued in natural science itself. But it is obvious, too, that the gift of seership leads beyond the immediate present. What is the way, the only way, of reaching out beyond the present? It is to have ideals. Ideals, however, are usually abstract: a person sets them before him and believes that they conform with the realities of the present. But instead of setting up abstract ideals, a person who desires to work in line with the aims of the supersensory world tries to discover causes lying in the womb of the ages, asking himself: how do these causes express themselves in the flow of time? He approaches this problem not with his intellect but with his deeper faculty of seership. True knowledge of the past—when this is acquired by the operation of deeper forces and not by way of the intellect—calls up before the soul pictures of the future which more or less conform with fact. And one who properly exercises the gift of seership today, after having pondered the stream of evolution in olden times, will find a picture rising up before him as a concrete ideal. This picture seems to tell him: humankind is standing at the threshold of transition; certain forces hitherto concealed in the soul are becoming more and more apparent. And just as today people are familiar with intellect and with imagination, so in a future which is by no means distant, a new faculty of soul will be there to meet the urge for knowledge of the supersensible world.

The dawn of this new soul power can already be perceived. When such images of what must happen in the future stimulate us, our attitude will not be that of the fanatic, neither will it be that of the pure realist, but we shall know why we do this or that for the sake of spiritual evolution. This, fundamentally, is the purpose of all true prophecy. We realize that this purpose is achieved even when the pictures of the future outlined by the seer may not be absolutely accurate. Anyone who is able to perceive the hidden forces of the human soul knows better than most that false pictures may arise of what the future holds in store; he understands, too, why the pictures are capable of many interpretations. To say that although certain indications have been given, they are vague and ambiguous, does not mean very much. Such pictures may well be ambiguous. What matters is that impulses connected with evolution as it moves on towards the future shall work upon and awaken slumbering powers in the human being. These prophecies may or may not be accurate in every detail; what matters is that powers shall be awakened in the human being.

Prophecy, therefore, is to be conceived less as a means of satisfying curiosity by prediction of the future than as a stimulating realization that the gift of seership is within the human being's grasp. There may well be negative sides— but the good sides are there too. The good side will be revealed above all when human beings do not go blindly through the day nor blindly onwards into a remote future but can set their own goals and direct their impulses in the light of knowledge. Goethe, who has said so many wonderful things about the affairs of the world, was right when he wrote the words: 'If a man knew the past, he would know what the future holds; both are linked to the present as a whole complete in itself.' (*Wer das Vergangene kennte, der wüsste das Künftige; beides schliesst an heute sich rein als ein Vollendetes an.*) This is a beautiful saying from the *Soothsayings of Bakis*.[24]

And so the *raison d'être* of prophecy does not lie in the appeasement of curiosity or the thirst for knowledge, but in the impulses it can give to work for the sake of the future. The unwillingness to be really objective about prophecy today is due to the fact that our age sets too high a value on purely intellectual knowledge—which does not kindle impulses of will. But spiritual science will bring the recognition that although there have been many negative sides in the realm of ancient and modern prophecy, nevertheless in this striving for awareness of the future a seed has formed, not for the appeasement of cravings for knowledge or of curiosity, but as fire for our will. And even those who insist upon judging everything in the human being by cold, intellectual standards must learn from this vista of the world that the purpose of prophecy is to stimulate the impulses of will.

Having considered how attacks against prophecy may be met and having recognized its core and purpose, we have a certain right to say: in this domain lie many of those things with which academic philosophy will have nothing to do. That is certainly true. But the light of this very knowledge will also reveal many facts which illustrate the other saying, that intellectual knowledge—however correct it may be—is sometimes completely valueless because it is incapable of engendering impulses of will. Just as it is true that there are many things undreamed of by philosophy, so on the other side it is true that a great deal in the realm of scientific research into the things of heaven and earth comes to nothing because it does not quicken the seed of right endeavour. But progress in life must be made in the light of a kind of knowledge which reveals that at the beginning, the middle and the end everything turns upon human activity, human deeds.

3. Cosmic influences on the individual and humanity

Here our relationship to the cosmos is set out—our life between incarnations and how we prepare a future life on earth according to these experiences with the cosmic spiritual forces, and how this becomes the basis for a horoscope. Although dismissive of much of what passed for astrology then, Steiner nonetheless gives the remarkable fact of how a person's brain reflects the starry pattern at his or her birth. Thus we have a basis for judging a horoscope if only we can read it correctly. The statement that 'if Mars is in Aries ... certain forces cannot pass through Mars but are weakened instead' *would appear to contradict the astrological tradition that a planet is strengthened if it is in the sign that it rules, namely Mars in Aries, and also that the sign in question is more prominent. In a later lecture included here (Dornach, 17 May 1924), Rudolf Steiner explains this further: the sign's forces are blocked by the planet, but the result is that the person must develop those forces in him or herself all the more—hence the result appears to be of a strengthened sign plus those planetary forces, i.e. a person with stronger Aries forces and an enhanced Mars.*

Christology is at the heart of Steiner's teachings and, as we shall see, this is no less significant for astrology and astronomy—the former especially is often viewed as 'pagan' and has been denounced by the Churches at many times during the past centuries. Here we are reminded of the mystery of Christ's incarnation—that there were at first two infants (more fully explained in other lectures)[25] and it was at the baptism that the Christ entered the combined Jesus being. Then we have the remarkable revelation that at every moment of Christ's life on earth the heavenly forces flowed through him, each moment was like a 'birth' in itself, and how much can be understood about the healings in the Gospels from this, as Christ manifested the cosmic healing forces.

The remainder of the lecture assists in placing these ideas into connection with the development of astronomy since the Middle Ages and how we continue to be guided by spiritual powers even if humanity has mostly lost the awareness of this.

To speak of Christ as the leader of successive worlds and of the higher hierarchies is the teaching of the science that has unfolded since the twelfth and thirteenth centuies under the sign of the Rose Cross, a science that has increasingly proven essential for humanity.[26] Looking at Christ from this perspective, we gain new insights into the being who lived in Palestine and then fulfilled the Mystery of Golgotha, as the following shows.

There have been many different views of Christ before today's. For example, certain Christian Gnostics of the first centuries claimed that the Christ who lived in Palestine did not have a physical body of flesh at all but had only an apparent—etheric—body that became visible to physical eyes.[27] Consequently, since for them only an etheric body was present, they said Christ's death on the cross was not a real death but only an apparent one. There were also various disputes among the adherents of Christianity—for example, the famous dispute between the Arians and the Athanasians[28] and so on—as well as many different interpretations of the true nature of Christ. Many different views of Christ, indeed, have been held by people right into our own time.

Spiritual science, however, must see Christ not just as an earthly being but as a *cosmic* being. In a certain sense, we human beings are also cosmic beings. We live a dual life: a physical life in the physical body from birth until death and a life in the spiritual worlds between death and rebirth. While we are incarnated in the physical body, we are dependent on the earth because the physical body is subject to the living conditions and forces of the earth. We ingest the substances and forces of the earth, and we are also part of the earth's physical organism. But once we have passed through the portal of death we no longer belong to the forces of the earth.

Yet it would be wrong to imagine that having passed through the portal of death we do not belong to any forces at all, for after death we are connected with the forces of the solar system and the other galaxies. Between death and rebirth we live in and belong to the cosmos in the same way as between birth and death we live in the earthly realm and belong to the elements of air, water, earth and so on. After death, we enter the realm of cosmic influences; for example, the planets affect us not only with gravity and other physical forces explained by physical astronomy but also with their spiritual forces. Indeed, we are connected with these cosmic spiritual forces after death, each of us in a particular way appropriate to our individuality. Just as a person born in Europe has a different relationship to temperature conditions and so on than a person born in Australia, so each of us similarly has a unique, individual relationship to the forces working on us during life after death. One person may have a closer relationship to the forces of Mars while another is more closely connected to those of Jupiter and yet others may have a closer relationship to the forces of the entire galaxy, and so on. These forces also lead us back to the earth to our new life. Thus, before our rebirth we are connected with the entire starry universe.

The unique relationship of an individual to the cosmic system determines which forces lead him or her back to earth; they also determine to which parents and to which locality we are brought. The impulse to incarnate in one place or another, in this or that family, in this or that nation, at this or that point in time, is determined by the way the individual is integrated into the cosmos before birth.

In the past the German language had an expression that poignantly characterized the birth of an individual. When someone was born, people said that he or she had 'grown young'. Unconsciously, this expression indicates that following death we are first subject to the forces that made us old in our previous incarnation, but just before our new birth these are replaced by other forces that make us 'young' again. In his drama *Faust*, Goethe says of someone that he 'grew young in Nebelland' (the land of mist); Nebelland is the old name for medieval Germany.[29]

People who are knowledgeable about these things can 'read' the forces that determine a person's path in his or her physical life; on this basis horoscopes are cast. Each of us is assigned a particular horoscope because it reveals the forces that have led us into this life. For example, if in a particular horoscope Mars is in Aries, this means that certain Aries forces cannot pass through Mars but are weakened instead.

Thus, human beings on their way into physical existence can get their bearings through their horoscope. Before ending this discussion—which, after all, seems a daring one in our time—we should note that most of what is presented today in this area is the purest dilettantism and pure superstition. As far as the world at large is concerned, the true science of these things has largely been lost. Therefore, the principles presented here should not be judged according to the claims of modern astrology, which is highly questionable.

The active forces of the starry world push us into physical incarnation. Clairvoyant perception allows us to see in a person's organization that he or she is indeed the result of the working together of such cosmic forces. I want to illustrate this in a hypothetical form that nevertheless corresponds fully to clairvoyant perceptions.

If we examined the structure of a person's brain clairvoyantly and could see that certain functions are located in certain places and give rise to certain processes, we would find that each person's brain is different. No two people have the same brain. If we could take a picture of the entire brain with all of its details visible, we would get a different picture for each person. If we photographed a person's brain at the moment of birth and took a picture of the sky directly above his or her birthplace, the two pictures would be alike. The stars in the photograph of the sky would be arranged in the same way as certain parts of the brain in the other picture. Thus our brain is really a picture of the heavens, and we each have a different picture depending on where and when we were born. This indicates that we are born out of the entire universe.

This insight gives us an idea of the way the macrocosm manifests in the individual and from this, in turn, we can understand how it manifests in Christ. If we were to think that after the baptism, the macrocosm lived in Christ in the same way as it does in any other human being, we would have the wrong idea.

Let us consider for a moment Jesus of Nazareth and his extraordinary life. At the beginning of the Christian era, two boys named Jesus were born. One belonged to the Nathan line of the house of David, the other to the Solomon line of the same house. These two boys were born at approximately—though not exactly—the same time.[30]

In the Solomon child portrayed in the Gospel of St Matthew, the individuality incarnated who had lived earlier as Zarathustra. Thus in the Jesus depicted in the Gospel of St Matthew we actually encounter the reincarnated Zarathustra or Zoroaster.[31] The individuality of Zarathustra grew up in this child just as Matthew describes it, until the boy's twelfth year. Then Zarathustra left his body and entered the body of the other Jesus, the one described by the Gospel of St Luke. That is why at this moment the child Jesus so suddenly became entirely different from what he had previously been. When his parents found him in the temple in Jerusalem after the spirit of Zarathustra had entered him, they were astonished. This is shown by the fact that they could not understand what he said when they found him for they knew only the Nathan Jesus as he had been before. The Jesus who now stood before them could talk as he did to the scribes in the temple because the spirit of Zarathustra had now entered into him.

The spirit of Zarathustra lived and matured to a still higher perfection in this Jesus, who came from the Nathan line of the house of David, up to his thirtieth year. It should also be noted that impulses from the Buddha streamed out of the spiritual world into the astral body of this youth, in whom the spirit of Zarathustra now lived.

It is true, as the Eastern tradition teaches, that the Buddha was born as a 'Bodhisattva' and only reached the rank of Buddha on earth in his twenty-ninth year.[32] When Gautama Buddha was still a small child, Asita, the great Indian sage, came weeping to the royal palace. As a seer, Asita knew this royal child would become the 'Buddha'. He only regretted that, since he was already an old man, he would not live to see the son of Suddhodana become Buddha. This wise man Asita was reborn in the time of Jesus of Nazareth; it is he who is introduced in St Luke's Gospel as the temple priest and sees the Buddha reveal himself in the Nathan Jesus. And because he saw this he said: 'Lord, now lettest thou thy servant depart in peace ... for mine eyes have seen thy salvation' (Luke 2:29–30). Through the astral body of this Jesus boy—the one presented in the Gospel of St Luke—Asita could see what he had not been able to see in India: the bodhisattva who has become Buddha.[33]

All of this was necessary for the development of the body that was to receive the baptism by John in the River Jordan. At the moment of the baptism, the individuality of Zarathustra left behind the threefold body—physical, etheric and astral—of the Jesus who had grown up in the complicated way that enabled Zarathustra's spirit to dwell in him, for the reborn Zarathustra had had to undergo the two developmental possibilities represented in the two Jesus boys. Thus John the Baptist was brought before the body of Jesus of Nazareth in whom the cosmic individuality of Christ was now working. Other human beings are placed into their earthly existence through cosmic-spiritual laws, but these are then counteracted by those originating in the conditions of the earth's evolution. In the case of Christ Jesus, however, the cosmic-spiritual powers alone remained active in him after the baptism. The laws of the earth's evolution did not influence him at all.

During the time that Jesus of Nazareth pursued his ministry and journeys as Jesus Christ in Palestine in the last three years of his life—from the age of 30 to 33—the entire cosmic Christ-being continued to work in him. In other words, Christ always stood under the influence of the entire cosmos; he did not take a single step without cosmic forces working in him. The events of these three years in Jesus' life were a continuous realization of his horoscope, for in every moment during those years there occurred what usually happens only at birth. This was possible because the entire body of the Nathan Jesus had remained susceptible to the influence of the totality of the forces of the cosmic-spiritual hierarchies that guide our earth.

Now that we know that the whole spirit of the cosmos penetrated Christ Jesus we may ask: who was the being who went to Capernaum and all the other places Jesus went? The being who walked the earth in those years certainly looked like any other human being. But the forces working in him were the cosmic forces coming from the sun and the stars; they directed his body. The total essence of the cosmos, to which the earth belongs, determined what Christ Jesus did. This is why the constellations are so often alluded to in the Gospel descriptions of Jesus' activities. For example, in the Gospel of St John the time when Christ finds his first disciple is described as 'about the tenth hour' (John 1:39). In this fact the spirit of the entire cosmos expressed itself in a way appropriate to the appointed moment. Such indications are less obvious in other places in the Gospels, but people who can read the Gospels properly will find them everywhere.

The miracles of healing the sick must also be understood from this point of view. Let us look at just one passage, the one that reads, 'Now when the sun was setting, all those who had any that were sick with various diseases brought them to him; and he laid his hands on them and healed them' (Luke

5:40). What does this mean? Here the Gospel writer points out that this healing was connected with the constellation of the stars, that in those days the necessary constellation was present only after the sun had set. In other words, in those times the healing forces could manifest themselves only after sunset. Christ Jesus is portrayed as the mediator who brings together the sick and the forces of the cosmos that could heal them at precisely that time. These were the same forces that also worked as Christ in Jesus. The healing occurred through Christ's presence, which exposed the sick to the healing cosmic forces. These healing forces could be effective only under the appropriate conditions of space and time, as described above. In other words, the forces of the cosmos worked on the sick through their representative, the Christ.

However, these forces could work in this way only while Christ was on earth. Only then were the cosmic constellations so connected to the forces in the human organism that certain diseases could be cured when these constellations worked on individuals through Christ Jesus. A repetition of these conditions in cosmic and earthly evolution is just as impossible as a second incarnation of the Christ in a human body. Thus, the life of Christ Jesus was the earthly expression of a particular relationship between the cosmos and human forces. When sick people remained for a while by Christ's side, their nearness to Christ brought them into a relationship to the macrocosm and this had a healing effect on them.

*   *   *

What I have said so far allows us to understand how the guidance of humanity has been placed under the influence of Christ. Nevertheless, the other forces whose development was held back in the Egypto-Chaldean epoch also continue to work alongside those that are Christ-filled, as we can see in many contemporary interpretations of the Gospels. Books are published that take great pains to show that the Gospels can be understood astrologically. The greatest opponents of the Gospels cite this astrological interpretation, claiming, for example, that the path of the Archangel Gabriel from Elizabeth to Mary represents the movement of the sun from the constellation of Virgo to another one.

To a certain extent, this astrological interpretation is correct; however, in our time, ideas of this sort are instilled into people by the beings whose development was arrested during the Egypto-Chaldean epoch. Under their influence there are some who would have us believe that the Gospels are merely allegories representing certain cosmic relationships. The truth is, however, that the whole cosmos is expressed in Christ. In other words, we can characterize Christ's life by describing for each of its events the cosmic relationships that, through Christ, entered life on earth.

As soon as we understand all this correctly, we will inevitably and fully accept that Christ lived on earth. The false view mentioned above, however, claims that, because Christ's life is expressed in the Gospels through cosmic constellations, it follows necessarily that the Gospels are only an allegory of these constellations and that Christ did not really live on earth.

Allow me to use a comparison to make things clear. Imagine every person at birth as a spherical mirror reflecting everything around it. Were we to trace the outlines of the images in the mirror with a pencil we could then take the mirror and carry the picture it represents with us wherever we went. Just so, we carry a picture of the cosmos within us when we are born, and this one picture affects and influences us throughout our lives. Of course, we could also leave the mirror clean as it was originally, in which case it would reflect its surroundings wherever we took it, providing us with a complete picture of the world around us. This analogy explains how Christ was in the time between the baptism in the Jordan and the Mystery of Golgotha. What enters our earthly life only at our birth flowed into Christ Jesus at each moment of his life. After the Mystery of Golgotha, what had streamed into Christ from the cosmos merged with the spiritual substance of the earth, and it has been united with the spirit of the earth ever since.

When Paul became clairvoyant on his way to Damascus, he was able to perceive that what had previously been in the cosmos had merged with the spirit of the earth. People who can relive this event in their soul can see this for themselves. In the twentieth century, human beings are able for the first time to experience the Christ-event spiritually, as St Paul did. Up to this century only those individuals who had gained clairvoyant powers through esoteric schooling were able to have such experiences. Today and in the future, however, as a result of natural human development, advancing soul forces will be able to see Christ in the spiritual sphere of the earth. Beginning with a certain point in the twentieth century, a few people will be able to have such experiences and will be able to relive the event at Damascus, but thereafter gradually more and more people will be able to do so, and in the distant future it will have become a natural capacity of the human soul to see Christ in this way.

*   *   *

When Christ entered earthly history, a completely new element was introduced into it. Even the outer events of history bear witness to this. In the first cultural periods after the Atlantean catastrophe, people knew very well that the physical planets, such as Mars, Jupiter, or Saturn, were the expressions or manifestations of spiritual beings.

In later ages this view was completely forgotten. People came to see the heavenly bodies as merely material things—to be judged according to their physical conditions. By the Middle Ages, people saw in the stars only what their physical eyes could perceive: the sphere of Venus, the sphere of the sun, of Mars, and so on up to the sphere of the firmament of fixed stars. Beyond that, they believed, there was the eighth sphere which enclosed the others like a solid blue wall around them.

Then Copernicus came and shook to its foundations the established outlook of relying completely and exclusively on what the human senses could perceive.[34] According to modern natural science, only people with muddled minds can claim that the world is maya or illusion and that we must look into a spiritual world to see the truth. Scientists believe that true science is based on what our senses tell us, and they record those perceptions. However, the only time when astronomers relied exclusively on their senses was in the days when the astronomy prevailed that modern astronomers oppose!

Modern astronomy began to develop as a science when Copernicus started to think about what exists in the universe beyond the range of human sensory perception. In fact, it is true of all the sciences that they developed in opposition to sensory appearance. When Copernicus explained that what we see is maya, illusion, and that we should rely on what we cannot see—that was the moment when science as we know it today began.

In other words, the modern sciences did not become 'science' until they stopped relying exclusively on sensory perception. Giordano Bruno, as the philosophical interpreter of Copernicus's teachings, proclaimed that the eighth sphere, which had been considered the boundary of space enclosing everything, was not a boundary at all.[35] It was maya, an illusion, and only appeared to be the boundary. In reality, a vast number of worlds had been poured into the universe. Thus what had previously been regarded as the boundary of the universe now became the boundary of the world of human sensory perception. We have to look beyond the sense world. Once we no longer see the world merely as it appears to our senses, then we can perceive infinity.

Originally, then, humanity had a spiritual view of the cosmos, but in the course of history this was gradually lost. The spiritual world-view was replaced by an understanding of the world based exclusively on sensory perception. Then the Christ impulse entered human history. Through this principle humanity was led once again to imbue the materialistic outlook with spirituality. At the moment when Giordano Bruno burst the confines of sensory appearance, the Christ development had so far advanced that the soul force, which had been kindled by the Christ impulse, could be active within him. This indicates the significance of Christ's involvement in human history and development, which is really still in its early stages.

What, then, are the goals of spiritual science?

Spiritual science completes what Bruno and others did for the outer physical sciences by demonstrating that the conventional, sense-based sciences can perceive and understand only maya or illusion. At one time, people looked up to the 'eighth sphere' and believed it to be the boundary of the universe. Similarly, modern thinking considers human life bounded by birth and death. Spiritual science extends our view beyond these boundaries.

Ideas like this one allow us to see human evolution as an uninterrupted chain. And, indeed, what Copernicus and Bruno accomplished for space by overcoming sensory appearance had already been known earlier from the inspirations of the spiritual stream that is continued today by spiritual science or theosophy. Modern esotericism, as we may call it, worked in a secret and mysterious way on Copernicus, Bruno, Kepler, and others. Thus, people whose outlook is based on the findings of Bruno and Copernicus betray their own traditions when they refuse to accept theosophy and insist on looking only at sensory appearance.

Just as Giordano Bruno broke through the blue vault of heaven, so spiritual science breaks through the boundaries of birth and death and proves that the human being comes from the macrocosm to live in this physical life and returns again to a macrocosmic existence after death. What is revealed in the individual on a limited scale can be seen on a much larger scale in the representative of the cosmic spirit, in Christ Jesus. The impulse Christ gave to evolution could be given only once. Only once could the entire cosmos be reflected as it was in Christ; the constellation that existed then will not appear again. This constellation had to work through a human body in order to be able to impart its impulse to the earth. Just as this particular constellation will not occur a second time, so Christ will not incarnate again. People claim that Christ will appear again on earth only because they do not know that Christ is the representative of the entire universe and because they cannot find the way to the Christ idea presented in all its elements by spiritual science.

Thus, modern spiritual science or theosophy has developed an idea of Christ that shows us our kinship with the entire macrocosm in a new way. To really know Christ we need the inspiring forces that are now imparted through the ancient Egyptian and Chaldean beings who were higher than human beings and who were themselves guided by Christ. We need this new inspiration, which has been prepared by the great esotericists of the Middle Ages since the thirteenth century. This new inspiration must now be brought more and more to the attention of the general public. If we prepare the soul properly for the perception of the spiritual world according to the teachings of spiritual science, we will be able to hear clairaudiently and to see clairvoyantly what is revealed by these ancient Chaldean and Egyptian powers, who have now become spiritual guides under the leadership of the Christ being. The first Christian centuries up to our own time were only the preparation for what humanity will receive and understand one day.

In the future, people's hearts will be filled with an idea of Christ whose magnitude will surpass anything humanity has known and understood so far. The first impulse that Christ brought and the understanding of him that has lived on until now is, even in the best exponents of the Christ principle, only a preparation for a true understanding of Christ. It would be strange, but is not beyond the bounds of possibility, that those who present the Christ idea in this way in the West could be accused of not basing themselves on western Christian tradition. After all, this western Christian tradition is utterly inadequate for understanding Christ in the near future.

Western esotericism allows us to see the spiritual guidance of humanity gradually merge with the guidance proceeding from the Christ impulse. Modern esotericism will gradually flow into people's hearts, and the spiritual guidance of the individual and humanity will more and more be seen consciously in this light.

Let us recall that the Christ principle first entered human hearts when Christ ministered in Palestine in the physical body of Jesus of Nazareth. In those days, people who had gradually resigned themselves to trusting only in the sensory world could receive the impulse appropriate to their understanding. The same impulse then worked through modern esotericism to inspire such great minds as Nicholas of Cusa, Copernicus, and Galileo.[36] That is why Copernicus could assert that sensory appearance cannot teach us the truth about the solar system and that we must look beyond it to find the truth.

At that time, people were not yet mature enough—even a brilliant man like Giordano Bruno was not yet ready—to integrate themselves consciously into the stream of modern esotericism. The spirit of this stream had to work in them without their being conscious of it. Giordano Bruno proclaimed proudly that the human being is actually a macrocosmic being condensed into a monad to enter physical existence; and that this monad expands again when the individual dies. What had been condensed in the body expands into the universe in order to concentrate again at other levels of existence and to expand again, and so on. Bruno expressed great concepts that fully agree with modern esotericism, even though they may sound like stammering to our modern ears.

We are not necessarily always conscious of the spiritual influences that guide us. For example, such influences led Galileo into the cathedral of Pisa. Thousands of people had seen the old church lamp there, but they did not look at it the way he did. Galileo saw the lamp swing and compared its oscillations with his pulse beats. In this way he discovered that the church lamp swung in a regular rhythm similar to that of his pulse—the 'law of the pendulum', as it is known in modern physics. Anyone familiar with modern physics knows that physics as we know it would not exist if it had not been for Galileo's laws. What was at work in leading Galileo to the swinging lamp in the cathedral—thus giving modern physics its first principles—now works in spiritual science. The powers that guide us spiritually work secretly in this way.

We are now approaching a time when we have to become conscious of these guiding powers. We will be able to understand better what must happen in the future if we correctly grasp the inspiration coming to us from modern esotericism. From this inspiration we also know that the spiritual beings whom the ancient Egyptians considered to be their teachers—the same beings who ruled as gods—are ruling again, but that they now want to submit to Christ's leadership. People will feel more and more that they can allow pre-Christian elements to be resurrected in glory and style on a higher level. In the present era we need a strengthened consciousness, a high sense of duty and responsibility concerning the understanding of the spiritual world. For this to enter our soul we must understand the mission of spiritual science in the way I have outlined.

4. The subtle impact of the stars

If the cosmic forces influence us, then how does this happen? This extract shows us how not *to view it. And further ones will show the way in which we bring into earthly life the results of our cosmic experiences in the spiritual world between incarnations.*

In the course of our present studies I should like it to become increasingly clear that the human being does not belong to the earth alone, to earth existence alone, but also to the cosmos, to the world of stars. Much of what there is to say in this connection I have, as you know, already said. I want now to begin with a brief remark in order that misunderstandings may be avoided.

Anyone who speaks of the human being's connection with the world of the stars is probably always liable to be accused of leanings towards the superficial form of astrology that is so widely pursued nowadays. But if what is said on this subject is rightly understood, the immense difference will at once be apparent between what is meant here and the amateurish interpretations of ancient astrological traditions that are so common today.

When we say that the human being between birth and death is a being connected with the earth and earthly happenings, what do we mean by this? We mean that the human being owes his existence between birth and death to the fact that, in the first place, he takes the substances of the earth into his metabolic system as nourishment and digests them; further, that through his breathing, and through the inner processes connected with his breathing, he is related in still another way to the earth—that is to say, to the atmosphere surrounding the earth. We also say that the human being perceives the outer things of the earth by means of his senses, and indeed perceives reflections of what is extraterrestrial— reflections which are, however, of a much more earthly character than is generally supposed. So that in general one can say: the human being participates in earthly existence through his senses, through his rhythmic system, and through his metabolic system, and has within him the continuation of the processes set in operation through earth existence itself.

But equally there takes place in the human being a continuation of cosmic, extraterrestrial processes. Only it must not be thought when it is said that an influence from the moon, or Venus, or Mars affects a person that this is to be understood merely as if rays of some kind are sent down from Mars or Venus or the moon and penetrate him. When, for instance, it is said that a person is subject to the influence of the moon, this must be taken as an analogy of what is meant by saying that a person is subject to the influences of the earth's substances. When someone passes an apple tree, let us say, picks an apple and eats it, it can be said that the apple tree influences him; but we should not interpret this so literally as to say that the apple tree had sent its rays towards him. Or, if you like, when a person passes a meadow where there is a bullock and a week later eats its meat, we shall not at once form the idea that the bullock has exercised some influence over him. Neither must we picture so literally what is said about the influence of the world of the stars on the human being. Nevertheless, the relationship between the world of stars and the human being and between the human being and the world of stars is just as much a reality as the relationship between the person and the bullock he passes in the meadow and the meat which he subsequently eats.

5. The human being as expression of the constellations and the planets

Rudolf Steiner was not simply dismissive of the old astrology, he was at pains to give a basis for both the ancient traditions and for a way of understanding that would lead into the future. In these extracts he considers the traditional correspondences of the human form with the twelve signs of the zodiac. He then relates the seven visible planets to inner movements, e.g. the blood, the breath, but in such a way that we do not simply think of physical planets, but more importantly of spiritual beings at work in their spheres—the actual planet in its motion delineating the boundary of the sphere. Thus we are led towards a new astrology which recognizes cosmic beings working from heavenly spheres to create and maintain the human form. In speaking of these, Steiner makes clear the importance of the moment of birth for realizing certain attributes. He was speaking to people who were members of the Theosophical Society in Oslo and assumes a certain background knowledge and understanding of occultism, but the lectures are worth penetrating for gaining a better grasp of what is still taught today about the relationship between the human form and the zodiac and planets.

To achieve greater precision, let us now study the human form in some detail. If we wanted to use scholarly language we would say, let us dissect the human form. When we do so, we are at once struck by the remarkable fact that the human form divides up quite naturally into various elements. We shall see clearly what these elements are when we enquire how the human being came to receive his present form. We shall find that the truths which are drawn from the deep wells of esotericism give us a complete picture of the division of the human form, show us how the human form has been put together.

The first thing to note about the human form, the first thing in this form that makes the human being what he is, is what I laid stress on in the opening words of these lectures, the fact that it is upright. The human being is a being who walks upright. That is the first important thing about him—the first element of his form—his upright posture.

It will perhaps seem to you as though there were something arbitrary about the way I am dissecting the human form. But if you follow closely and carefully, you will see that it is not really so at all; the fact is, the essential human being as described for us in esoteric knowledge is reflected in his form or figure.

The second thing that makes the human being what he is and that will also be readily recognized as essential to the human form is the fact that he is so constituted as to enable him to be a speaking being. Sound can be born in him. Consider how essential a characteristic this is. In general, the human being is organized in an upward direction, and in particular he is so organized that his speech organs, beginning from the heart and larynx, go upwards to the face. Study the human being from this aspect and you will find that all the forms of the limbs are so arranged as to suit the creation and forming of spoken sound. Thus we can say, the second important factor in the structure of the parts of the human form is that they are ordered and disposed with a view to speech.

The third thing that we have to regard as important for the form of the human being is the fact that it is symmetrical. It is hard to imagine that the human form would not lose something of its real nature if it were not symmetrical. That then is the third essential, that the limbs and parts are symmetrically disposed. As we know, there are exceptions, but the quality of symmetry is essential.

The fourth thing to consider manifests in the following way. If you observe these three first sections of the human form—upright posture, speaking, symmetry—you will see that they are all directed outwards. The fact that the human being holds himself upright is something that places him into the external world. Speech is again something that obviously relates him to the external world. Finally, the symmetry of his form gives him a certain balance in space. Now we come to a different aspect. We come to the fact that the human being has an inside. From the purely physical point of view the human being has organs that are enclosed within his skin. We may, therefore, say that the human being has as the fourth part of his form the fact of enclosure within the skin, so that the organs on which the inner functions depend are inside and are protected from the external world. Enclosure or isolation within the skin is thus something that properly belongs to the human form.

To find the fifth section of the human form, you must understand that within it, in the parts that are shut away from the outside, we find organs, active inner organs. All that lives and works inside the human being—that is the fifth thing we have to note. That there is movement and life within him can convince us that the human being as he stands before us in his form is not just dependent on the external world, but is also dependent on his own inner human being as well; he has within him what might be described as a focal point for the flow of his being. Contrast, for example, the circulation of the blood with the sections we have already described. There you have a process that takes its course entirely inside the human being; it is something completely isolated from the world outside. Thus we have as fourth part the fact of enclosure or isolation, and as fifth, the inside of the human being that is so enclosed.

But now there is something further we have to observe about this inside of the human form. Looked at from the purely physical aspect, it is a duality. There are, first of all, organs like the lungs and heart, which owe their form to a compromise, for they are also subject to outside influences. Even the heart, by reason of its connection with the lungs, has to be adapted to outside conditions. The air from outside enters into the human being through the lungs and is by this means brought into contact with the inner organs. Then we have, on the other hand, organs which show by their form that they are adapted solely and entirely to the inside of the body. These are the organs of the abdomen. They owe their very shape and form to the fact that they are inside the human being. It is quite possible to imagine that the stomach, intestines, liver or spleen, if they were differently formed, could still be in connection with the heart and lungs and in some way or other fulfil their right and proper functions. When once the external world has found entrance into the lungs, then all the inner organs can assume their own several forms. They are determined entirely from within. So that we may say we have, as number six, a part of the human form which we may call the true inside of the human being in the physical sense. It is important to understand that here we have a part of the human form which has no connection with the outside world.

We have now come to a boundary in the human form,

where the outward direction begins to work again, where once more we find something that has a strong relationship to the outside world. Consider the shape of the human foot. If it were not formed for the ground, if it did not have a sole, the human being would not be able to walk. If his foot, for example, ended in a point, he would be continually falling down. Thus, as we follow the human form downwards, we come again to organs that are adapted for external conditions. At the same time we note that the feet, and also the legs, help to give the human being his distinctively human form. If the human being were a fish, or if he were a creature that flies in the air, these organs would have to be formed quite differently; as it is, their form expresses the fact that the human being is a being who stands and walks on the earth. All the organs from the hips downwards are shaped for this purpose—that the human being is a being able to work and stand and walk upon the earth. So that we may say, in the hips we have, as seventh part, a certain equilibrium. What is above is either given an outward direction in its form or, as we have seen, turned inwards; what is below is formed in a downward direction. In the hips we have a certain point of equilibrium. All that comes below is adapted to earthly conditions.

Then we have as eighth section organs that are entirely orientated to conditions outside the human being—the organs of reproduction.

Continuing further, a little reflection will enable you to see that for the human being to walk in the way that is proper to him, the thigh must be separate from the leg, there must be the bend between them. And so he has, joined on to the thigh, the knee, making it possible for him to adapt himself in his walk to earthly conditions. For it is earthly conditions that essentially determine the lower part of the shape of the human being. Then we have the lower leg and, separated again from it, the foot.

1. Upright posture
2. Utterance of Sound
3. Symmetry
4. Enclosure
5. Enclosed interior
6. Interior in physical respect, not related to outside world
7. Equilibrium
8. Reproductive organs
9. Thigh
10. Knee
11. Lower leg
12. Feet.

So just take a look at this list. As I said before, it might at first sight appear arbitrary to show the human form divided in this way into twelve parts. But everything the human being requires in his form in order for him to be a human being on earth is really contained in these twelve parts and in such a way that each part has a certain independence, each part is separate from the others. One could even imagine that each one of them, while remaining still in connection with the others, might assume quite another form from the form it actually has. It is perfectly possible in each single case to imagine other shapes or forms for these various parts, but that the whole human figure stands before us as the result of the conjunction of twelve such parts is a fact that cannot be disregarded.

When you reflect upon the whole meaning and purpose of

the human being's existence upon earth, you cannot leave out of account that he has a form and figure structured in this particular way, so that when we come to study this form we must inevitably think of it as divisible into twelve parts. These twelve parts have always been regarded from an esoteric perspective as of the deepest possible significance. We must take them into consideration if we want to understand the meaning of the form and figure of the human being in its relation to his being. Esotericism has always known of them, and for reasons which will become clear to us in the course of these lectures—as we continue our study of the human being from an esoteric, philosophical and theosophical perspective—we will see why these twelve elements were given very specific designations in a given context.

The first element has been designated as 'Ram' (Aries) and is denoted by the sign ♈.

The second is named the 'Bull' (Taurus) and symbolised with the sign ♉.

Symmetry is called 'Twins' (Gemini) and is denoted with the sign ♊.

What we described as the quality of enclosure within itself is given the sign ♋ and called 'Crab' (Cancer).

What we described as the interior, as enclosed life, is called 'Lion' (Leo) and symbolized with the sign ♌.

The inner parts of the human being that physically have no connection at all with the outside world and point to the threefold character of the human being's nature, themselves typifying complete isolation from the outside world, are called 'Virgin' (Virgo) and denoted with the sign ♍.

Then we come to the state of balance and here no explanation is needed for giving it the name 'Scales' (Libra) ♎.

The reproductive organs, which once again have an outward direction, are denoted by the expression 'Scorpion' (Scorpio) and symbolized with the sign ♏.

The thighs, designated 'Archer' (Sagittarius), have the sign ♐.

The knees, as 'Goat' (Capricorn), are symbolized with the sign ♑.

The lower leg is 'Waterman' (Aquarius) and has the sign ♒.

And finally, the feet are termed 'Fishes' (Pisces) and have the sign ♓.

For the moment, you should consider these signs as no more than signs and signatures for the various elements that go to make the complete human form. Regard them as nothing other than a tool, like choosing letters, to designate the various elements of the human form. Then you have done enough for the moment to observe what we designate as the human form. And because we separate it into its individual parts we can assign the listed names to those parts, we can give the individual elements the signs, like letters, which are set out next to them.

You all know that these signs correspond to ancient customs and in particular that they play a part in astrology. I want you, however, to connect nothing else with them now than the fact that with their help we are able to study the human form and see how it lends itself naturally to division into twelve elements. If it should seem that we are giving rather strange names and signs to these parts of the human form, it is really no different to the sounds of human speech where we cannot always immediately recognize why they express a particular thing; or as it is with the letters of the alphabet, of which we are often quite unable to say why they designate one thing or another.

What we have achieved with these designations is to find an expression for the twelve-part structure of the human being and to give these elements names for further use which have here and there found their way out of esoteric into general use.

It will now also be apparent to you on what the fundamental principle, the real essence of astrology is based. I say this because I do not intend to speak about astrology in great detail—there would not be time—but I want at this point to call your attention to its true nature. We can put it in a very few words.

There is a correspondence between the elements of the human form and the fixed stars, so that their signs can be ascribed to these various elements of the human being's form. Thus we have the human being complete in his physical form. But the influence proceeding from the powers that work from these directions was not active only when the human form first came into being, it has continued so right through time and is active still. And we see the working of this influence in the fact that the human being's external destiny can be brought into connection with the constellations of the stars, just as we have to connect with the constellations of the stars what the human being has already become. If it was auspicious for the human being's organization that his sun forces cooperated with those elements of his form to which we ascribed the sign of Leo, then it will also be auspicious today for certain qualities and characteristics in him if some important moment of his life, notably the moment of birth, falls when the sun is in the sign of Leo—that is to say, when the sun covers Leo, so that these two forces mutually strengthen or in some way influence one another. Just as what the human being is today stands written in the heavenly spaces in the writing of the constellations of the stars, so stands written there too what is yet to happen with him. This is the basis of true astrology. You will see at once from what we have been considering that you really only need to have a thorough knowledge of esotericism in order to have at the same time the principle of astrology, because we will now go on to describe the second stage of initiation.

We have seen that in order to attain to the first stage of initiation it is important for the pupil to take his start from the human form, from the human being as he presents himself to physical sight. For the next stage he has to choose something else as his starting point, namely the inner movement of the human being. Note carefully the distinction:

First stage: Starting from the human form.
Second stage: Starting best from the inner movement of
               the human being.

Let us now consider, as previously we considered the form or figure of the human being, the movements that take place within him. We have first of all a movement which, although in later life the human being scarcely performs it any more, had once to be carried out by him with all his strength, otherwise he would remain a four-footed creature, obliged to crawl on the ground for the rest of his life. The human being has to perform the movement which changes him from a crawling child to an upright being. For the human being is not merely an upright being by nature of his form; he is a being who during his life lifts himself upright. So that the first inner movement the human being performs—for it is an inner movement—is the movement of lifting himself into the upright position.

The second movement of an inner kind is again one that the

human being must acquire for himself as a child, although he continues to use this movement throughout life. It is the motion of speaking, the motion of the inner life that has to be performed for the word to be created. You must realize that a whole sum of inner movements is necessary in order that the word may be brought to expression. There is, however, still another movement, a more hidden one, that has also to be learned in early childhood. We may say, the human being learns both movements together. As a matter of fact, he basically learns the speaking movement earlier than the other. You will find a more precise and detailed account of all this in my little book *Education of the Child*.[37] We have, then, these two inner movements that the human being learns and has to perform throughout his life. We are quite aware of the speech movement. Everyone knows that they are doing it. But not everyone knows that when they think, a delicate movement is taking place all the time in their brain. To discover this requires a rather fine and subtle power of observation. I am not talking materialism when I refer to a 'movement'. Because the movement in the brain already exists; but it is effect and not cause. We therefore have two inner movements, the movements of thinking and of speaking.

If then we go further, we discover the movement of the blood as the next important motion required for the inner life of the body to take place. This is one of the movements which must necessarily take place for the human being to be a human being. The sequence is apparently rather arbitrary with regard to this movement, but that does not matter.

The fifth movement, which must already be there in order for the blood movement to take place, is the movement of the breath. This is a specific movement with an independent existence of its own, distinct from the movement of the blood. As I said, the sequence is somewhat arbitrary. We could, for instance, interchange the second and the third— but that is beside the point; here again we could put the breath before the blood movement, and if we were considering more especially the lungs we would certainly have to do so. If, however, we are looking rather to the origin of the movements, then we must take them in the sequence I have given; because, especially in the case of the male, the real centre and origin of the breath movement is in the diaphragm, and that is underneath the heart. When, therefore, our object is to build up a sequence from the point of view of origin, we have no choice but to take the movements in the sequence I have given.

The sixth movement—we are still speaking of movements inside the body that are necessary to life—is one that certain inner organs have to perform; we may summarize it in a general term and call it glandular movement or movement of vessels. The vessels in the human being's body must be in perpetual activity, perpetual inner movement, to maintain the life of the human being. For certain reasons which it would take too long to explain, I prefer to call it simply movement of the glands.

For the seventh movement to come about, it is no longer a question merely of particular vessels or glands moving in order to secrete something the human being requires within himself. The seventh is a movement performed by the whole body as such, and it is carried out when nature has set all in motion for a new human being to be born. What we have here is really a sum total of all the movements of the body. Whilst in other vessel or gland movements we have the movement of a part only of the body, in the case of the movement of reproduction we have a kind of act of secretion performed by the whole human being. And the same is true whether we are speaking of the male or female body. It is always a secretion performed by the whole human being. This movement then we call the movement of reproduction.

If the seven movements we have described are correctly understood, then they represent all the inner movements. The others are outer movements. When the human being moves his feet or his hands, that is an external movement. The human being brought the inner movements with him when he came to earth, though earth has, it is true, changed them very much. And just as we relate the whole complete form of the human being to the fixed stars of the zodiac, and connect the signs of the zodiac with the various elements of the human form, we now find that these various movements have their source in the entire planetary system.

We derive these seven elements of the human inner movement from our planetary system. And since the relationship of these movements in the human being to one another corresponds to the relationship of the planets in our planetary system, we can also designate these various movements with the signs that belong to the planets:

Movement into upright posture	♄	Saturn
Movement of thinking	♃	Jupiter
Movement of speaking	♂	Mars
Movement of the blood	☉	Sun
Movement of the breath	☿	Mercury
Movement of the glands	♀	Venus
Movement of reproduction	☽	Moon

With regard to the movement of the blood, this movement comes into contact with what we have earlier learned to recognize as the centre of the organs belonging to the middle human being, the contact area for the sun spirit. Thus the movement of the blood, which has its centre in the middle human being, must be related to the most important force in the middle human being, and we have to designate this movement of the blood with the sign of the sun. This is the power and force of the sun spirit in so far as it is a force in movement. It is, we could say, as a fixed star that the sun works upon the middle human being as a whole. On the other hand, it exerts its influences on the movements that depend on the middle human being, on the movements of the blood, as one of the planets.

If I make use of the signs which are also used by astronomers today—in this case therefore not employing the old terminology which was altered by Kepler[38] but the names that are customary in astronomy today—then the movement of the breathing can be denoted by Mercury ☿, the movement of the glands by Venus ♀, and the movement of reproduction by the moon ☽. This last movement, localized as it is in the lower human being, is again a movement that comes into contact with the influence of the spirit of the moon which engages here with the lower human being and touches his inner mobility.

When the esoteric aspirant removes himself from his being of inner movement, as has been described, when he steps out of his inner moving being, he encounters seven figures. He meets seven spiritual beings and he knows that these seven spiritual beings correspond to his own inner movements in the same way that the sun, moon and Venus correspond to what we discussed here yesterday and today. He comes to understand that he himself has grown out of our planetary system, and that the planets as physical celestial bodies are governed by planetary spirits, and that the human being is only able to lift himself upright because the spirit of Saturn is at work in him, the spirit who is located on Saturn just as Lucifer is located on Venus. The esoteric aspirant also knows that his movement of thought is connected with the regent or guiding spirit of Jupiter, the movement of speech with the guiding spirit of Mars, the movement of the blood with the guiding spirit of the sun, the whole movement of the breath with the guiding spirit of Mercury, all the glandular movements with the guiding spirit of Venus, and finally the whole movement of reproduction with the guiding spirit of the moon. He knows, furthermore, that all these spirits work with and through one another. They have their main seat, their active base, in the human being, and one kind of movement works on another. The spirit of Saturn, for instance, while it works chiefly through the movement made by the human being in lifting himself upright, takes part indirectly in all other movements. A significant situation occurs when the guiding spirit of Saturn manifests his forces with particular strength in Aries or Taurus. This creates a particularly significant situation.

Having thus come to the recognition of how the guiding spirits of the planets are connected with the various elements of the human being of inner movement, you will be able to follow me when I say that in the allocation of the signs to the various elements we are already touching the fundamental principle of all genuine astrology. You only need to know the connections we have been considering, and you will recognize that there lies inherent within them the principle of true and genuine astrology, which has its source in nothing else than in the great and significant fact that the human being is born out of the cosmos, that the human being is an essence, an extract of the whole cosmos.

6. Understanding the human form out of the universe

Steiner approaches the relationship of the human being to the zodiac in a different way here. He builds up the connections by considering certain basic gestures and stances, and then the earliest human activities. It is an unusual approach but one which encourages an inner mobility instead of offering a merely schematic view.

When he speaks of certain constellations as being 'covered by the earth' this is meant simply at any one time for of course the zodiac appears in constant rotation in relation to the earth. Speaking of 'being in the sign of the Fishes', he is speaking of the cultural epochs as designated by the zodiac, which will be described more fully in a later lecture. This threefold way of presenting the human form should not be imagined as being a contradiction to the previous one; Steiner was always at pains to present ideas from as many different perspectives as possible. The designations are the same but a much fuller concept is arrived at. It is a difficult lecture but worth the effort of study, especially the idea of metamorphosis from one lifetime to the next.

Today, we will consider the human form and we shall see how much this will add to our subject matter and deepen it. The first thing to remember is that, taken in its widest sense, the human form is of course connected with the whole of human life, and this is what we have to consider if we want to gain real inner understanding of it. Human beings are part of the whole universe, the cosmos. If you take it that the form of the human head primarily reflects the sphere of the cosmic universe, you may say that with regard to the head human beings relate to the whole universe. However, to understand how human beings relate to this when at the same time they are also an entity that is complete in itself, we have to consider the way human beings relate to the world around them.

Let us begin by saying that in all their thinking, in so far as it is connected with the head, human beings turn to the whole cosmos. When at birth we bring the head into this physical world from the world of the spirit we are encased in a living physical body and in a way able to look back to our inner reality of soul and spirit, and to a time when we were not encased in a body. It may be easiest to see what I mean if we consider how human beings gain insight and knowledge by looking back inside themselves, as it were. We are looking back inside ourselves, for instance, when we do arithmetic or geometry. We recognize the laws of geometry simply because we are human beings and are able to find the laws of physical space in ourselves. We also know that these laws fill the whole universe. This, then, is something we inevitably see when we use our eyes; everything is arranged in geometrical order. Even the design of our eyes, and the way we are able to focus, is based on geometry.

Thus we are able to say that when we relate to the world through thinking, which is connected with the head, we take back into ourselves what lies spread out in the universe. One way we relate to the universe may therefore be seen as follows: the universe is reaching into us, and we are, in a way, looking back on it. This would be the way in which human beings relate to the universe, out of which they have been built, at the most superficial level.

We progress a little more if we now consider, in second

place, how human beings make everything they take in from outside come alive in them. You see, when a child is born everything it went through between death and rebirth is inside it. If the child were able to develop the right kind of awareness, it would be able to look back on life before birth. Those pre-birth experiences then begin to stir. Human beings do not merely look back inside themselves to find the universe, but also look around them and see their environment. We are thus able to say: apart from taking in the universe, we also look out into the universe around us, taking its mobility into us. We become inwardly mobile.

Now to the third aspect. In the first two, human beings are not really quite inside themselves. Having the universe inside us, say as geometry, we live in something that is really outside us. When the child begins to be inwardly mobile as it imitates the movements of the universe, it lives in something that is outside it. How does the human being become inward and become aware of self?

Just take your left hand in your right hand, thoughtfully— all you have to do is take hold of yourself and you remain entirely inside yourself. You are using your right hand for an activity, but it is you yourself you take hold of. You may take hold of other objects at other times, but in this case you take hold of yourself. All self-awareness, all inwardness, essentially is a matter of thus taking hold of oneself. We do something similar with our eyes. When we focus on a particular point, the right visual axis intersects with the left visual axis, just as the right hand takes hold of the left. Animals have less inwardness because they do much less of this taking hold of self. The third thing, therefore, would be experiencing or touching ourselves. There we are actually in the outside world and take hold of ourselves, and we are not yet inside our skin.

Let us now consider the boundary between outside and inside. We indicate the process by letting the right hand move to and fro over the left hand which it is holding. This defines a surface area we actually have all over, the covering which encloses everything inside. The fourth thing, then, is to enclose oneself. Get a real feeling for the way the skin encloses your form, and there you have the closing-off principle.

1. The universe reaching in. Looking back
2. Looking out into the universe. Taking in the mobility of the universe
3. Experiencing self, touching self
4. Enclosing ourselves.

These four things show how the human being is gradually given form from outside in. First there is the whole universe and we are outside ourselves; then imitation of the universe, where we have not yet come to ourselves. Taking hold of ourselves we find ourselves outside ourselves. With the fourth element we enclose ourselves.

For the fifth we have to look for something that is inside us, fills us, actively pulses inside us.

As to the sixth, since we not only have a skin but also something that fills it we are now inside ourselves, but this is also where the form is dissolved again; we have something that not merely fills us inside, but makes us like a fruit when it grows ripe. Take a fruit when it is just on the point of being ripe; once it goes beyond this point it starts to dry up. The sixth thing, then, is ripening.

But visualize this ripening process. As we grow ripe we begin, in a way, to decay inwardly. We cease a little bit to develop further as human beings. We are human but we decay inwardly, turning to dust, as it were. We become mineral and thus part of the outside world again. That which fills us is wholly inside. But as we fall to dust we become part of the mineral world again. We become a body that has weight, as it were. The seventh thing, then, is to become part of the inorganic world.

I have shown, on another occasion, that if we weigh a human being who walks this earth, that human being is just like a mineral. There we have the process of becoming part of the forces of outer nature. Just think—if you walk properly you involve yourself in the forces of physical nature, and if you do not walk properly you fall over. The first step in finding our place in the outside world is therefore to find our balance.

The eighth thing: we find that we do not merely become part of the outside world but also take it into ourselves as we breathe and when we eat. Before, we essentially only fathomed things that were already inside ourselves; it is a matter of being alive inside. But we take the outside world into ourselves, and at this point it has to be clearly understood that everything we take in from outside is something that does not really belong inside us.

People have the wrong idea about the way we take in things from outside. In principle, everything we eat is a little bit poisonous. Life consists in taking in food and not letting it become entirely part of ourselves, resisting it. This resistance, defending ourselves, is in fact life. The point is, however, that the foods we eat are not very poisonous so that we are able to hold our own against them. If we take in real poison it will destroy us, for we will not be able to defend ourselves.

Thus we may say: with the outside world, a poison sting

enters into us. I have to use words that have real meaning, but today's language and understanding does not have them. You will have to understand what I mean when I put these things before you.

5. Something that fills us
6. Ripening
7. Becoming part of the inorganic world. Finding our balance
8. Poison sting.

The human being is now at the point where the outside world is taken in. First we considered the way the human being is given form out of the universe. Then came the way the human being is given form from inside, and this has taken us to where the inner human being gains form by resisting the outside world.

But human beings create their form, or at least shape their lives and a little bit also their actual human form, according to the way they relate to and are active in the outside world. Today our activities no longer relate entirely to our human nature; we have to go back to earlier times to see human beings relating to the world around them in a way that makes them act in a truly human way. We are then able to say that in the ninth place, one human activity is to involve oneself in the outside world here on earth, and not in the universe. In their outside life in civilization people were first of all hunters.

They progressed by developing another activity—breeding of animals. That is the tenth stage, and the eleventh stage of perfection is to be a tiller of the soil. Finally the twelfth stage is to be involved in trade. You will see later why I do not include other activities that followed. They were secondary. Hunting, animal breeding, tilling the soil and trading are the primary human activities. This, then, defines the human form in relation to the earth:

9. Hunter
10. Animal breeder
11. Tiller of the soil
12. Trader.

We might also show this in a drawing. Let us say this is the earth, and here we have the human being on earth. With regard to the first four form principles, form is given from outside, from the cosmos surrounding the earth (Fig. 1).

Let us leave the middle principle aside for the moment and consider where the human being is formed by the earth to be hunter, animal breeder; here the opposite would be the case. Here the constellations influence the human being; but the

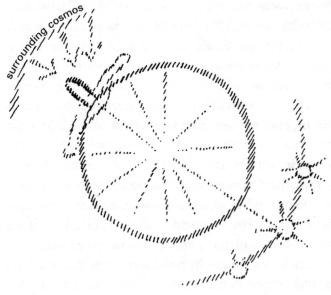

Fig. 1

influence of the constellations which are down there has to pass through the earth to reach the human being. This would mean that the human being would have to take his orientation from the earth where these stars are concerned. And the four middle principles would give human beings the potential to develop inwardly.

Thus these four principles (table, next page) take us out into the universe; the last four take us to the earth, with the stars involved covered by the earth. In the four middle principles, stars and earth are in balance, and we have human beings with an inner life.

People had a feeling for this in the past. They would say: one part of the starry heavens influences human beings by forming them from outside, out of the universe. Different stars had to be seen in that role through the ages, of course, for the constellations change. But let us take, broadly speaking, the age in which we live. An ancient Greek who had given some thought to these things would say: the stars that are in the region of the Ram are acting on us from outside, and so do those in the region of the Bull, the Twins and Cancer. Through them human beings have the principle in them that looks back, the one that is inwardly mobile, the one that takes hold of itself and the one that encloses itself. To the stars down there on the opposite side, which are covered by the earth, human beings owe their existence as hunters (Archer), animal breeders (Goat), tillers of the soil—walking across the field carrying urns to water the fields (Water Carrier). And we are traders thanks to the part of the starry heavens that takes us across the seas—in far distant times boats were built to look similar to fish, and two ships side by side that have sailed the seas in pursuit of trade are the symbol for trade. If we take the liberty and call the ships 'fishes' we have the twelfth sign.

The human being formed out of the universe—head

1. Taking in the universe	
Looking back	Ram
2. Looking out into the universe	
Taking in the mobility of the universe	Bull
3. Taking hold of ourselves (touch)	Twins
4. Enclosing ourselves	Crab, Cancer

The human being formed from within—chest

5. That which fills	Lion
6. Ripening	Virgin, with ear of corn
7. Becoming part of the inorganic world. Seeking balance	Scales
8. Poison sting	Scorpion

Forms of human activity on earth—limbs or earthly human being

9. Hunter	Archer
10. Animal breeder	Goat
11. Tiller of the soil	Water Carrier
12. Trader	Fishes

In the middle we have that which fills, that is, something which acts like the blood that fills human beings. The best animal to symbolize the blood is probably the Lion, because there we have the activity of the heart at its highest. Ripening—we only need to look at a field where the wheat or rye is getting ripe; the ear of corn is exactly the stage at which fruiting becomes ripening—so we have the Virgin with the ear of corn, and it is the ear of corn that matters. Human beings become part of the outside world again in seeking balance—Scales. And where we feel the poison sting, and feel that everything is slightly poisonous—Scorpion.

In the past, people really had a feeling for the way the human being is connected with the universe and the earth. In our time people say: Ram, Bull, Twins, Crab, Lion ... and draw those figures, but they no longer have any real idea as to their meaning.

It is important to see these things in the right way. If you look at an old illustration of the Ram, you'll realize that it is not a naturalistic, materialistic image of a ram. The important characteristic is, again and again, the gesture of looking back. The way the Ram looks back is the way the human being looks back on himself as he looks back to the universe that lives in him. It is the gesture that counts.

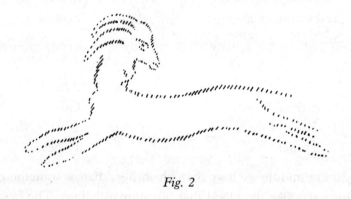

Fig. 2

If you look at old pictures of the Bull you will find that the Bull always looks sideways and makes a leap. It is the gesture of looking around you and letting the general, universal principle come alive in you. Looking at the Twins you have one person on the right and another on the left, and always the right hand of the one on the right holds the left hand of the one on the left. This is the gesture of touching, feeling oneself. Two individual persons are shown in order to indicate that in a way the human being is still outside himself, and takes his pre-birth human being into himself by touching himself.

Closing off, enclosing oneself—Crab. The people who chose the Crab as the symbol for this enclosing gesture did so because the crab puts its claws around its prey. The word 'cancer' actually still holds the meaning of enclose. The Crab is the symbol of the individual closing himself off, not merely touching and feeling himself but closing himself off from the outside and creating an inside.

The Lion is the animal of the heart, for the obvious reason that its heart is particularly well developed. It represents the qualities that come in fifth place.

With the quality of ripening, it is the ear of corn the Virgin holds that represents the fruiting quality when it is just on the point of drying up. The Scales show the search for balance, and the Scorpion is of course the poison sting. The Archer is really an animal form, the front part of which is a human figure with bow and arrow, like a Centaur astride an animal body. This is the hunter.

Capricorn, the he-goat, is really a goat with a fish's tail, something which does not exist in the natural world. But human beings breed animals and thus make them as tame as tame fish. This, then, is a made-up symbol.

Agriculture is represented by the Water Carrier. There is a certain spiritual justification for thinking in terms of water, but what matters is the way he walks across the field. He holds an urn in each hand and pours water from these. This is the gardener and the tiller of the soil.

I have already suggested that the Fishes represent trade.

People used to have fishes' heads up on the front part of their ships, heads of dolphins, for instance—dolphins are not fish, of course, but the ancients thought them to be. This symbol clearly points to trading activity.

Rather than consider these things in a superficial, schematic way, which is so often the case today, we have to look at the way the human being is given form and then see how this gives us the relationship to the universe and to the earth. Basing ourselves on the form, we gradually perceive the human being as part, as a member, of the whole universe.

Another approach is the following. Let us take the Ram, for instance. Considering Ram, Bull, Twins, Crab, Lion, Virgin, Scales, Scorpion, Archer, Goat, Water Carrier and Fishes from the point of view of the ancient Greeks we may say: in the shape of the head, the human being is formed out of the universe. Then mobility develops inside and the potential for symmetry. Next, however, it will be necessary to see the influence of the last constellations in the list as having the opposite effect. In this case the influences come from the earth. Activities have an effect on human beings.

If we made the figure broad at the top (see Fig. 3), we had

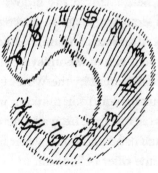

Fig. 3

best make it narrow (down) here, saying: when human beings want to be hunters the qualities we may take to be those of the Archer must be particularly well developed in them. To be animal breeders they have to bend their knees a lot. The tiller of the soil has to walk; he is therefore shown stepping out, and so on. Carrying on trade: if we want to look for a symbol in the human being, it has to be the feet. All these organs are also formed from outside in. The remaining part, where the human being develops himself, is in the middle.

This figure I am drawing really arises from the twelve signs as if of its own accord. We are able to say: there (in the middle) the universe with its stars is more active in the inner human being; there (at the top) the stars act from outside, and there (below) they compress the human being. You can see that the form I have drawn is the human embryo. Basing yourself on the laws of the zodiac, you really have to draw the human embryo like this, just as you get a triangle if you draw a figure that encloses 180 degrees. It is therefore immediately apparent that the human embryo is created out of the whole universe.

As I said, we have to take the point of view of the ancient Greeks to do this, for today we can no longer start with the Ram; we have to start with the Fishes. We have been in the sign of the Fishes for centuries now, and this marks the time of transition to human intellectual development. But if you go back to the time when it was right to start with the Ram and the zodiac could be seen the way the ancients saw it, you have not much more than Archer, Goat, Water Carrier and Fishes, or the occupations of the hunter, animal breeder, tiller of the soil and trader. Today we live in the age of the Fishes, during which the whole of our modern industrialized civilization has developed. Going back to the time of the

Ram, we still find the four honest occupations—though modified to some extent and more complex—which place human beings in the world of nature.

Going back through the ages of the Bull,[39] the third, second and first post-Atlantean ages, the last Atlantean age, the last but one, and so on, we would come to an earlier age of the Fishes, when human beings were still completely etheric and had not yet descended into the physical world. And because human beings were completely etheric in the earlier age of the Fishes, they are today essentially repeating everything they went through at that earlier time when they were in the process of becoming human. They have been repeating this from the middle of the fifteenth century, but in an abstract way. Then they were truly evolving their humanity; now they are growing into things that have been abstracted from them, for a machine is something that has been abstracted. With the new age of the Fishes, human beings are placed in something that is actually dissolving them. And when humanity enters another Water Carrier age, the process of dissolution will go a great deal further. Above all, human beings will not be able to relate to the world in any way at all unless they hold to the world of the spirit. It is exactly because of this recapitulation that humanity must move on into the world of the spirit.

Again it is possible to see that human beings are really threefold by nature: formed out of the universe in so far as they are head; developing inwardly, merely in concord with the outside world, in so far as they are chest; developing limbs and metabolism in so far as they make themselves part of the physical world, i.e. are limb people, or earth people (see table on page 86).

Threefoldness exists also in another respect. When we

arrive in the world, the first four powers or impulses are already in us, though we only develop them afterwards. Yet in a sense we are also full human beings, for the potential for the other eight principles is also there. The head person is a whole human being, but the other parts are only rudimentary. The chest person is a whole human being, but the first and last four impulses are rudimentary. The limb person is a whole human being, but chest and head are rudimentary. So we really have three people in every human being. The first, the head person, is a metamorphosis of the previous incarnation. The chest person is the human being of the present incarnation in the true sense. And everything we do in the world around us, which comes to expression in our limbs and in our metabolism, takes us forward into our next incarnation. In this way, too, human beings are threefold by nature, and it is another way of studying the human form as a whole.

We really ought to say that to draw a human being we ought to draw the head. This would be a complete human being. You can see it like this: the lower jaw really represents legs, except that in the head they point backwards; this person is sitting on his legs.

The chest person is another whole human being, with the arms more or less the outer representatives of etheric eyes. And the limb person is another whole human being, with the kidneys the eyes, for example. Even in terms of form and shape, we have three human beings fitted into one another. In the human being who has vanished into the head and become a sphere we see the previous incarnation coming alive, in the chest we have the actual human being of the present time, and in the person who is walking about we may see what will enter into the next incarnation.

In a sense we are also able to say that the way people

comport themselves today shows a threefold nature. Take the human being of the limbs and metabolism: he is capable of engendering a whole human being. All you need is the human embryo in the mother's womb and you see how the limbs and metabolism person wants to become a whole human being.

As to the chest person, look at a small baby and you can see how at that stage the head and chest still form a whole. Threefoldness therefore shows itself also in the way we grow up. And when we are no longer babies we are brought up and educated. The human head is the educator of other human beings—a child's head, or a childish person, teaching another childish person, for essentially we are for ever children in the head. We only grow old, that is to middle age, in the middle or chest person, and really old in our limbs. People find out about this when they get old. As the old riddle goes: we walk on all fours in our youth, then on two and later on three legs. People grow old in their limbs. In their head they always remain somehow the outcome of their previous incarnation, and throughout life the head is really a child's head. Education theory will have to solve the problem of how the child's-head teacher can best treat the child's-head pupil.

These things can be amusing, but behind them lies a deep truth which must be considered if human beings are to see themselves in the right light.

Essentially the human head is a passenger carried by the rest of the human being. The legs of the head are always in a sitting position and it does not even attempt to do its own walking. The head is carried around like a passenger sitting in a coach. The chest person is the carer, and the limb person is the worker, used as slave, and the one who really works his way through life. This is also why we have a head, in so far as we are head as a whole human being; I have said so many times. All the way to where we enclose ourselves, using the Crab principle, we are head. This is the gift of heaven and we do not have to contribute. Here (in the middle) we must breathe and eat: this is the carer, the wet-nurse. And the true worker belongs to the sphere of Archer, Goat, Water Carrier and Fishes.

We are thus able to evolve the human form in relation to the whole universe. You need to take these things very seriously, even if they are presented with a fairly light touch and not in a pedantic way. Taking them seriously you will see that on the one hand everything I have said today holds the potential for understanding the human form out of the whole universe, and on the other hand it is something to make us feel the greatest respect for the perceptiveness of people in the past; out of instinctive clairvoyance they were able to gain the most tremendous knowledge of the human being from the signs of the zodiac. Today our knowledge is such that people goggle at the Ram but fail to realize that the way it turns around is the important thing; they goggle at the Bull and do not know that it is the way it leaps and looks sideways that matters; and with the Twins the way one hand holds the other, and so on. Everything in those signs of the zodiac, every single gesture, is truly profound, and if there is no gesture, as in the case of the Lion, the symbolic element has been chosen in such a way that the sign itself has the gesture in it, with the Lion having the strongest heart beat. The Lion represents that which fills us. We can find the wisdom of those ancient days again if we look for it in ourselves.

7. The changing vision of the universe

This short passage emphasizes the need to understand planets and stars in terms of spiritual beings, a knowledge which humanity once had but then lost. Steiner's vast output of lectures was given to enable us to make these connections anew in a conscious way beginning with our thinking forces.

We can look back from this world conception to ancient times when the prevailing picture of the universe was very different. All that has remained of it are those traditions which in the form in which they exist today—in astrology and the like—are sheer dilettantism. That is what has remained of ancient astronomy, and it has also remained, ossified and immobilized, in the symbols of certain secret societies, Masonic societies and the like. There is usually complete ignorance of the fact that these things are relics of an ancient astronomy. This ancient astronomy was quite different from that of today, for it was based not upon mathematical principles but upon ancient clairvoyant vision.

Entirely false ideas prevail today of how an earlier humanity acquired its astronomical and astrological knowledge. This was acquired through an instinctive clairvoyant vision of the universe. The earliest post-Atlantean peoples saw the heavenly bodies as spirit forms, spirit entities, whereas we today regard them merely as physical structures. When the ancient peoples spoke of the celestial bodies, of the planets or of the fixed stars, they were speaking of spiritual beings. Today, the sun is pictured as a globe of burning gas which radiates light into the universe. But for the people of ancient times the sun was a living being and they regarded the sun, which their eyes beheld, simply as the outward manifestation of this spirit being at the place where the sun stands in the universe; and it was the same with regard to the other heavenly bodies—they were seen as spirit beings. We must think of an age which came to an end long before the time of the Mystery of Golgotha, when the sun out yonder in the universe and everything in the stars was conceived of as living spirit reality, living Being.

Then came an intermediary period when people no longer had this vision, when they regarded the planets, at any rate, as physical, but still thought of them as pervaded by living souls. In times when it was no longer known how the physical passes over by stages into what is of the soul, how what is of the soul passes over by stages into the physical, how in reality the two are united, people postulated physical existence on the one side and soul existence on the other. They thought of the correspondences between these two realms just as most psychologists today—if they admit the existence of a soul at all—still think, namely that the soul and the physical nature of the human being are identical. This, of course, leads to some absurd thoughts; or there is the so-called 'psycho-physical parallelism' which again is nothing else than a stupid way of formulating something that is not understood.

Then came the age when the heavenly bodies were regarded as physical structures, circling or stationary, attracting or repelling one another in accordance with mathematical laws. To be sure, in every epoch there existed a knowledge—in earlier times a more instinctive knowledge—of how things are in reality. But in the present age this instinctive knowledge no longer suffices; what in earlier times was known instinctively must now be acquired by conscious effort. And if we enquire how those who were able to view the universe in its totality—that is to say, from a physical, soul and spiritual perspective—if we enquire how these people pictured the sun, we must say: they pictured it first and foremost as a spirit being. Those who were initiated conceived of this spirit being as the source of all that is moral.

8. The forces of the planets

Rudolf Steiner spoke of the way in which planets are connected to human life in various ways. Here we have a very clear exposition of how these forces can affect us in our subtle bodies—but also how, and in this he would differ from a traditional astrological perspective, we can free ourselves—especially in relation to Saturn. We can actually feel in ourselves the 'nerviness' induced by the wrong relationship here, due to the prevailing intellectual bias of our time. Since the 1920s this increase has been manifold due to technological advances and it is difficult for us to appreciate the effects of computers and other devices on our nervous system, which bears the physical connection to our astral body.

What does Steiner mean when he says that in order to have a stronger thinking capacity, a person must choose to be born when Jupiter is sending its rays down directly? What follows here is a passage from an earlier article by the compiler in an attempt to explain this with reference to Jupiter's cycle:

'. . . It would seem that Steiner is referring to something other than a daily rhythm—Jupiter rising or culminating—traditionally 'significant' positions at birth. Unless we are in extreme latitudes all planets rise and set each day and thus shine down directly from the sky even if not visible because it is daylight. But in winter the sun is much lower in the sky and visible for a shorter length of time than in summer, because the earth's axis is inclined at an angle with respect to the ecliptic. Planets, likewise, have their 'seasons' in accordance with their own cycles. Joachim Schultz describes Jupiter's cycle thus:

The twelve-year period of Jupiter's progression through the zodiac may be thought of as a 'Jovian year' by analogy to the solar year. During this period the arcs of Jupiter's daily motion rise and sink; and its direction of rising and setting change. During a solar year roughly the same metamorphosis takes place in Jupiter's diurnal arcs as for those of the sun in a month. Over a period of six years, when Jupiter is moving through the upper portion of the zodiac, it ascends to relatively high culminations, as for example from 1987 to 1992, and again from 1999 to 2004. In addition there is a period of especially good visibility during the oppositions, at which time Jupiter, owing to its high position in the zodiac, is above the horizon for more than twelve hours. During the following six years we find Jupiter in the lower constellations of the zodiac. It remains close to the horizon in the southern sky. Its visibility is less favourable and of a shorter duration.[40]

'*The regions of the zodiac wherein the highest culmination and greatest visibility of Jupiter take place are of course not the same as for the sun. But it can be seen from the dates given that in northern latitudes the area of maximum visibility is when Jupiter is moving from sidereal (i.e. the actual constellation) Pisces through to Virgo, and the less favourable period is when it passes from Libra back to Pisces. So it is significant for the development of the capacity for wisdom to be born when Jupiter has still to move through the zodiac somewhere between Pisces and Virgo, the closer to Pisces the better. It is not easy to check such a statement statistically because it would be difficult for people to determine what is the maximum capacity for wisdom. Such a person may in fact seem slow or not obviously successful, but has however a truly creative and original approach. An example of a person with "Jupiterian" thinking would be Goethe, with his remarkable output of both literary and scientific works. At his birth, Jupiter was near the beginning of sidereal Pisces and therefore during the six years following his birth it would have been in the optimum position. It appears that it was not "necessary" for Jupiter to be actually rising or culminating at birth.*[41]

We simply take earthly life today as the basis of our ideas and concepts and construe a view of the whole universe in accordance with conditions on earth. The resulting picture of the universe is then not much else than the transference of earthly conditions to extraterrestrial ones. Thus, by means of the tremendous achievements of modern science, through spectral analysis and other methods, a view of the sun was developed that is really modelled entirely upon earthly conditions. A conception is formed of what a luminous body of gas might look like. This conception is then transferred to what meets our eye as the sun in the cosmos. We must once again learn to use the materials of spiritual science to arrive at a conception of the sun. The physicist believes that the sun would present itself to him as a luminous sphere of gas if he were able to travel out into space. Yet, despite the fact that it reflects the cosmic light to us in its own way in the manner it receives it, the sun is a spiritual entity through and through. We are not dealing with a physical entity that moves about somewhere out there in the universe but with a completely spiritual being.

The Greeks still had the right feeling when they experienced the light, shining down upon them from the sun, as something that must be brought into a connection with their ego development in so far as this ego development is tied to the conceptual nature of the intellect. The sun's rays were to the Greeks something that enkindled their ego within them. It is therefore obvious that the Greeks still had a feeling for the spirituality of the cosmos. To them, the sun being was substantially a being related to the ego. The element the human being becomes aware of when he says 'I' to himself, the force that works in him and enables him to say 'I' to himself, this is what the Greeks looked at. They felt called upon to address the sun in the same way they addressed their ego, to regard the sun with the same feelings they had for their ego.

Ego and sun are the inner and the outer aspects of the same being. What orbits out there through space as the sun is the cosmic I. What lives within me is the human I.

One is inclined to say that this sensation is still faintly perceptible to those who have a somewhat deeper feeling of affinity for nature. The basis of such an experience has already vanished to a large degree. Yet, something is still alive in the human being today that is attuned to the rise of the sun in springtime, that can still experience the spirituality of the sunbeam and can feel how the ego is imbued with new life when the rays of the sun illuminate the earth with greater intensity. Yet, it is but a last, faint sensation that, even in this external manner, is dying out in mankind. It is about to disappear in the abstract, shadowy culture of the intellect that has gradually become prevalent in the whole of civilized life today. However, we must once again reach the point where some recognition can be gained of humanity's relationship with supersensible existence. In this respect I want to point out a number of things today.

By bringing together all the references found here and there in anthroposophical literature, we shall be able, first of all, to comprehend once more the sun's connection with the ego. We shall be able to perceive the significant contrast between the forces radiating from the sun to the earth and those forces that are active in what we term the moon. Sun and moon are in a certain respect total opposites. Complete polarity exists between them. When we study the sun by means of spiritual science, we find that the sun sends down to us everything that fashions us into bearers of our ego. We owe to the rays of the sun what in fact bestows on us the human form and, in the latter, moulds us into an image of the ego. What works in the human being from outside and determines his form from without even as early as the embryonic stage are influences from the sun. When the human embryo is developing in the womb, a great deal more is taking place than what present-day science is dreaming about, namely, that forces originate from the impregnated mother that then develop the human being. No, the human embryo merely rests in the mother's body; it is given form by the sun's forces. It is true, however, that we must bring these sun forces into connection with the moon's forces that have opposite effects. The moon forces become evident, above all, as the inner influence in the lower, metabolic nature of the human being. In drawing an outline, we may therefore say: the sun's forces are the element moulding the human being from outside. What develops in the metabolic processes from within are the moon's forces, positioning themselves within the human organism and radiating outward from the centre.

This does not contradict the fact that these moon forces also play a part, for instance, in forming the human countenance. They shape the face because the effects that proceed from the centre, from the lower, metabolic system, exert an attracting power, as it were, from outside on the development of the human face. The moon forces have a differentiating effect on this development due to adding their influence to that of the sun's forces while counteracting the latter from

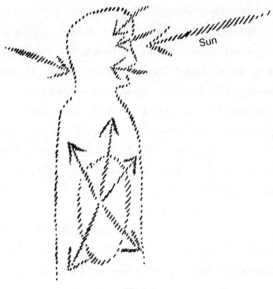

Fig. 4

within the human being. For this reason, the organism
connected with human reproduction depends on the moon
forces, which bestow the form. On the other hand, the result
of procreation depends on the sun forces. With their whole
being human beings are placed into the polarity between sun
forces and moon forces.

In seeking the moon forces within the inner human
organism, we have to distinguish them in the metabolic
process from the forces originating within this process itself.
The moon forces play into the metabolism but the latter
possesses its own forces. These are the earth forces. The
forces contained in food substances, in vegetables and other
foods, work in the human being by virtue of their own nature.
Here, they are active as earth forces. Metabolism is primarily
a result of the earth's forces, but elements of the moon's
forces work into them. If the human being possessed only the

metabolic process with its forces, if only the substances of his foods would unfold their forces in his body after having been consumed, then he would have nothing but a chaotic play of all kinds of forces. The fact that these forces continuously work to renew the human being from within does not depend at all on the earth; it is due to the moon that is added to earth. The human being is shaped from within outwards by the moon, from without inwards by the sun. Inasmuch as the sun's rays are received through the eye into the human head organization, they also have an inward effect; nevertheless, they still work from outside in.

Thus, on the one hand, in regard to his whole ego development the human being depends on the influence of the sun; without the sun he could not be an ego dwelling solidly on the earth. On the other hand, there would be no human race, no propagation, if the moon were not the earth's companion. It is possible to say that it is the sun that firmly places the human being as a personality, as an individual, on the earth. It is the moon that conjured human beings in their multitude, in their whole evolution, upon the earth. The human race in its physical succession of generations is the result of the moon forces, which stimulate human beings. The human being as a single being, an individuality, is the product of the sun forces. Therefore, if we wish to study the human being as well as the human race, we cannot study merely the conditions of earth. Geologists seek in vain to investigate the earth's conditions in order to comprehend the human being; they study in vain the other forces of earth so as to arrive at this understanding. Human beings are not primarily a creation of the earth. They are formed out of the cosmos; they are the offspring of the world of the stars, above all, of sun and moon. From the earth, only those forces are derived that are contained in matter itself. They are effective outside the human being and then continue their effects when, through eating and drinking, they have entered into the human being, but there they are received by something that is of an extraterrestrial nature.

The processes that take place within the human being are by no means merely earthly ones; they are definitely something provided for out of starry worlds. It is this insight that human beings have to struggle to attain once again.

When we observe the human being further, we can take into consideration, first of all, that he is a physical body. This body absorbs the external foods. They in turn extend their forces into this physical body. But the latter is also taken hold of by the astral body, and in it the moon's influence is active in the manner I have just described. The sun's effect also plays into this astral body. Imbuing it with their forces, sun and moon permeate the astral body, and the latter works in the manner I have outlined above. The etheric body stands in the middle between physical and astral body.

When we study the forces coming from foodstuffs, we find, to begin with, that they are active in the physical body, and, in the manner I described earlier, are then taken hold of by the astral body containing the sun and moon influences. But in between the physical and astral bodies we find something else that is active in the etheric body. It, too, is not derived from the earth but from the whole surrounding cosmos. When we study the earth with its products in relation to the human being, the substances composed of solid, liquid, or aeriform ingredients, we see that they are consumed by the human being and then worked upon by the forces of sun and moon. In addition, there are also active in the human being forces that stream in from all directions of the universe. The forces

active in the foodstuffs come from the earth. Those streaming into the human being from all corners of the universe are
the etheric forces. They also take hold of the foodstuffs, but
in a much more uniform manner, and transform them in
such a way that they become inwardly capable of life. In
addition, the etheric forces turn these foodstuffs into something that can inwardly experience the etheric element as
such, namely, light and warmth. Thus, we can say that
because of his physical body the human being is part of the
earth, because of his etheric body he is related to the whole
surrounding sphere, and because of his astral body the
human being is connected above all with the effects of moon
and sun.

Now, these effects of moon and sun contained in the astral
body are in turn modified. They are modified to the extent
that a powerful difference exists between the effects upon the
upper human organization and those on the lower human
organism.

Let us refer today to the part of the human being that is
permeated by the bloodstream flowing upwards towards the
head as 'upper human organization'; let us refer to what lies
below the heart as 'lower human organism'. In viewing the
human being thus, we have, first of all, the upper part
including his head and whatever is organically connected
with it. Its formation is dependent mainly on the sun's effects
and also develops first during embryonic life. Already in the
embryo, the sun's effects work on this organization in a quite
special way, but these effects then continue after birth when
the human being is present physically in the life between birth
and death. Roughly speaking, what lies in this part of the
human organism above the heart—a more detailed description would have to trace the blood circulation above the

heart—is then modified in regard to the astral influences by Saturn, Jupiter and Mars (see outline p. 112).

According to the Copernican world-view, Saturn has forces it develops in its orbit around the sun and then sends down to the earth. It possesses those forces that are effective in the whole human astral body, particularly in the part belonging to the above-mentioned upper organism of the human being. Saturn possesses the forces that stream into this astral body. As these forces penetrate and enliven the latter, they essentially determine the extent to which the astral body places itself in a proper relationship to the physical body. When a person cannot sleep well, for example, when his astral body does not properly emerge from the etheric and physical bodies, when it does not correctly re-enter them upon awakening, or in some other way does not fit itself properly into the physical body, then this is an effect, but an irregular one, of the Saturn forces. Saturn is chiefly the celestial body that, by way of the human head, brings about a correct relationship of the astral body to the human physical and etheric bodies. By means of this, on the other hand, it is the Saturn forces that produce the connection between astral body and ego because of Saturn's relation to the sun. This relationship of Saturn to the sun's effect is expressed in regard to space and time in the fact that Saturn completes its orbit around the sun in a period of 30 years.

In the human being this relationship of Saturn to the sun comes to expression in the ego achieving an appropriate relationship to the astral body and, above all, in the proper incorporation of the astral body into the whole human organization. Thus we can say Saturn possesses a relationship to the upper part of the whole human astral body. This relationship was definitely an important factor for people in ancient times. Even in Egypto-Chaldean times, going back to the third and fourth millennium prior to the Mystery of Golgotha, we would find that among the teachers, the sages in the mysteries, every individual was judged according to how he had determined his relationship to Saturn by the date of his birth. For these wise men knew quite well that depending on whether a person was born during one or another of Saturn's celestial positions, he was one who could use his astral body in the physical body in a more efficient or less efficient manner. Insight into such things played an important role in ancient times. The progress of human-kind's evolution, however, is denoted precisely by the fact that in our age, which, as you know, began in the fifteenth century, we are freeing ourselves of the influences affecting us there.

My dear friends, do not misunderstand this. It does not mean that Saturn is not active in us today. It works in us just as it did in antiquity; the point is that we have to free our-selves from it. And do you know in what this freeing our-selves in the proper way from the Saturn influences consists? You free yourself most poorly from the Saturn influences if you follow the shadowy intellect of the present time. In doing so you actually permit the Saturn effects to run riot within yourself, to shoot hither and thither, and actually to turn you into what is nowadays called a nervous person. A nervous condition in a person is caused mainly by the fact that the astral body does not fit properly into the whole physical configuration. The nervousness of our age is due to this. Human beings must be induced to strive for real perception, for imagination. If they remain with abstract conception, they will become more and more nervous, for they are actually growing out of the Saturn activity, which is nevertheless within them, shooting back and forth, pulling the astral body out of the nerves, thus making people nervous. In a cosmic sense, the nervousness of our age has to be recognized as an effect of Saturn.

Just as Saturn is chiefly involved with the upper part of the whole astral body inasmuch as the latter is connected with the whole organism through the nervous system, so Jupiter is active in thinking (see outline p. 112).

Human thinking, after all, is also based in a certain way on a partial activity of the astral body. I should say, a smaller part of the astral body is active in thinking than in sustaining the whole human being. It is Jupiter's effect that works in our astral body and, above all, strengthens our thinking. The effect of Jupiter deals mainly with the astral permeation and organization of the human brain.

Now, Saturn's effects actually extend over the whole of adult human life after the first three decades of our life. For our whole life and health depend on how we develop in our astral body during the periods of growth, and in fact, they only cease after age thirty. That is why Saturn requires thirty years to circle around the sun. This completely fits the human being. The thinking that develops in us has to do with the first twelve years of life. After all, what orbits out there in space is not without a connection to the human being.

Just as Jupiter has to do with thinking, so Mars has to do with speech.

Saturn	upper part of the whole astral body
Jupiter	thinking
Mars	speech

Mars separates a still smaller part of the astral body from its incorporation into the remaining human organization than the one that comes into play in regard to thinking. And it depends on the Mars effects within us that the forces can unfold that then pour into speech. The small revolution of Mars also has a bearing on this. A human being acquires the first sounds of speech within a time span that corresponds roughly to half the Martian orbit around the sun.

Ascending and descending development! We see how this whole development is linked with the forces of Saturn, Jupiter, and Mars in so far as it is tied to the region of the human head.

We have thus considered the outer planets' activity in the human astral body. Whereas the sun is connected more with the ego, these three cosmic bodies, Saturn, Jupiter, and Mars, have to do with the development of what is tied to the astral body, namely, speech, thinking, and the whole conduct of the human soul in the human organism.

Besides the sun, which has to do with the actual ego, we also have in addition those planets called the inner planets. They are the ones that are closer to earth than the sun, having their place between earth and sun, whereas, seen from the earth, the other planets, Saturn, Jupiter and Mars, are on the other side of the earth from the sun.[42] When we focus on these inner planets we likewise arrive at a consideration of the connections between their forces and the human being. To begin with we shall consider Mercury.

Similar to the moon, Mercury has its target points more in the inner being of the human being, working from outside only on the human countenance. In the part lying below the region of the heart, its forces are effective by taking hold inwardly of the human organization and, in turn, streaming forth from there. Mercury's chief task is to bring the astral body's activity into all breathing and circulation processes of the human being. Mercury is the intercessor between the astral body and the rhythmic processes in the human being. Thus, we are able to say that its forces intercede between the astral element and the rhythmic activity. Due to this, similar to the moon forces, the Mercury forces also intervene in the whole human metabolism, but only in so far as the metabolism is subject to rhythm, reacting to rhythmic activity.

Then there is Venus. Venus is active especially in the human etheric body, in what works out of the cosmos in the human etheric body and its activities.

Finally we have the moon, which we have already mentioned. It is the element in the human being that is the polar opposite of the sun forces. From within, it leads substances into the realm of life and therefore is also connected with reproduction. In the fullest sense, the moon stimulates inner reproduction as well as the procreative process of reproduction.

You realize now that what actually takes place in the human being is becoming evident to you in its dependence on the surrounding cosmos. On the one hand, with the physical body, the human being is tied to the earthly forces. On the other hand, he is linked to the whole cosmic environment with his etheric body. In that body, differentiations occur in the manner I have just outlined, and inasmuch as the differentiation proceeds primarily from the human being's astral body, the forces of Saturn, Jupiter, Mars, Mercury, Venus and moon integrate themselves into this body. By way of the ego, the sun is also active in the human being. Now take into consideration that due to the fact that the human being is integrated into the cosmos in this manner, it makes a difference whether a person stands at a given spot on the earth, and Jupiter, for instance, shines down on him from the sky, or whether he is in a location where Jupiter is covered by the earth. In the first case, Jupiter's effects on the person are direct ones; in the second case, the earth is placed in between. This results in a significant difference.

Saturn	upper part of the whole astral body
Jupiter	thinking
Mars	speech
Sun	ego
Mercury	mediation of the astral elements with the rhythmic activity of the human being
Venus	activity of the human etheric body
Moon	stimulator of reproduction

We have said that Jupiter is connected with thinking. Let us assume a person receives the direct Jupiter influence during the period when his physical organ of thinking is in the stage of major development after birth. His brain will be formed into a quite special organ of thinking; the person receives a certain predisposition to thinking. Assume that a person spends these years in a place where Jupiter is on the opposite side of the earth, the latter thus hindering Jupiter's influences. Such a person's brain is less developed into an organ for thinking. If, on the other hand, the earth with its substances and forces is active in a person and everything proceeding from them is transformed, say, by the moon influences, which in a certain sense are always present, such a person turns into a dull dreamer, one who is barely aware. Between these two possibilities we find any number of variations.

Let us take the case of an individual possessing forces from his former incarnation that predestine his thinking to develop in a pronounced way in the earth life on which he is about to embark. He is on the verge of descending to earth. Since Jupiter has its set time for completing its orbit, he chooses the moment when he is to appear on earth, when he is to be born, so that Jupiter sends down its rays directly.

In this manner, the starry constellation provides the setting into which the human being allows himself to be born, depending on the conditions of his former incarnations.

Today, in the age of the consciousness soul,[43] the human being must free himself increasingly from what is becoming evident to you here. It is a matter, however, of freeing oneself from these forces in the proper manner, of actually doing something I have indicated in regard to the Saturn effects, namely of trying to turn once again from the mere shadowy, intellectual developing of thoughts to a pictorial, concrete one. What is developed on the basis of spiritual science in the way I described it in *Knowledge of the Higher Worlds*[44] is also a guideline for human beings to become independent in the right way from the cosmic forces that are nevertheless active in them.

It depends on the starry constellations how a human being finds his way into earth life as he allows himself to be born. Yet he has to equip himself with forces that make him independent in the right way from this starry constellation.

9. The spiritual individualities of the planets

Always at pains to reveal inner soul qualities in outer nature and lead away from the abstract, Steiner here describes the planets as if they were characters in a drama. We also hear more of Jupiter's connection to thinking. The planets are allowed to come alive for us and we can begin to put together a renewed understanding of their forces. The idea of 'liberating and of destiny determining' planets would be a fresh challenge for the traditional astrologer.

I want to add to what has previously been said some explanation of certain deeper foundations of world mysteries of which all knowledge has been lost in modern civilization. To realize the loss we need think only of the modern conception of the planetary system: that it originated in some kind of rotating, primeval nebula, from which the various planetary bodies were dispersed. The speculations derived from this picture have led merely to the idea that there are no fundamental differences between these heavenly bodies, and this is the prevailing attitude towards them.

If the whole planetary system is comprised in the picture of a rotating nebula, out of which the heavenly bodies gradually separated, what essential difference is there between, for example, the moon and Saturn? It is of course true that very important researches carried out during the nineteenth century into earthly substances—particularly the minerals— have been able to say a great deal about the material composition of the heavenly bodies, and have worked out a certain kind of physics and chemistry for them. This has made it possible for ordinary textbooks to give specific details about Venus, Saturn, the moon, and so on. But all this amounts to no more than making an image of—let us say—the physical organism of the human being, leaving out of account altogether the fact that he is a being of soul and spirit. With the help of initiation science we must again learn to realize that our planetary system, too, is permeated with soul and spirit. And today I want to speak of the 'individualities' and the individual characters of the several planets.

We will think, to begin with, of the planet nearest the earth, the planet with whose history the earth's history—though only in a certain sense—is bound up, and which once played an entirely different part in earthly life from the part it plays today. You know from my book *Occult Science—an Outline*[45] that there was once a cosmic age—relatively speaking not in a very remote past—when the moon was still united with the earth. The moon then separated from the earth and now circles around it.

When we speak of the moon as a physical body in the heavens, its physical nature is only the external, the most external, revelation of the spiritual behind it. To those who have knowledge of both its outer and its inner nature, the moon in our universe presents itself to begin with as a gathering of spiritual beings living in great seclusion. Outwardly, the moon acts as a mirror of the universe; the fact that it reflects the light of the sun is evident to the most superficial observation. So we can say: what comes from the moon is the light of the sun which has shone upon it and is then reflected. First and foremost, then, the moon is a mirror of the sun's light. Now, as you all know, we see what is outside or in front of a mirror but we do not see what is behind it.

The moon is not the mirror of the sun's light only, for it

reflects everything that radiates upon it—the sun's light being, of course, by far the strongest. All the heavenly bodies in the universe send their rays towards the moon, and the moon—as a mirror of the universe—then radiates them back in every direction.

It can be said, therefore, that the universe is before us in a twofold aspect. It reveals itself in the environment of the earth and is radiated back by the moon. The sun's rays work with tremendous power in themselves and also in their reflection from the moon. But every other radiation in cosmic space is also reflected by the moon. There is the manifested universe and there is also its reflection from the moon.

Anyone capable of observing the mirrored images thrown back by the moon in all directions would have the whole universe before him in reflection. Only that which is within the moon—that and that alone—remains, if I may so express it, the moon's secret; it remains hidden, just as what is behind a mirror remains hidden. What is behind the outer surface of the moon, in the innermost sphere of the moon, is significant above all in its spiritual aspect.

The spiritual beings populating this innermost sphere of the moon are beings who shut themselves off in strict seclusion from the rest of the universe. They live in their moon 'fortress'. And only someone who, by developing certain qualities connected with the human heart, succeeds in relating himself to the sun's light in such a way that he does not see the reflection from the moon—only for such a person does the moon become inwardly transparent, as it were, and he can penetrate into this moon fortress of the universe. He then makes the significant discovery that through the utterances, through the teachings, of those beings who have withdrawn into seclusion in this moon fortress certain secrets can be revealed that were once in the possession of the most advanced spirits on the earth but have long since been lost.[46]

The farther we go back in the evolution of the earth, the less do we find the abstract truths that are the pride of present-day humanity. More and more we find truths expressed in pictures. We grapple with the deeply significant truths still preserved as a last echo of oriental wisdom in the Vedas and the Vedanta philosophy until we come to the primal revelations hidden behind the myths and sagas, and we realize with wonder and awe that a glorious wisdom was once possessed by human beings who received it without intellectual effort as grace from the spiritual worlds. And finally we come to all that was once taught to primeval humanity on earth by the beings who have now withdrawn into the moon fortress in the universe, after leaving the earth together with the moon. A certain memory was preserved of what these beings had once revealed to the peoples of a remote past—to human beings whose nature was quite different from human nature as it is today.

If we succeed in fathoming this mystery—I will call it the moon mystery of the universe—we realize that these beings who have now entrenched themselves in the moon fortress were once the great teachers of earthly humanity; but all consciousness of the realities of spirit and soul hidden in this fortress has been lost. What is still transmitted to the earth from the heavens represents only what the outer surface, the walls as it were, of the moon fortress radiate back from the rest of the universe.

This moon mystery was one of the deepest secrets in the ancient mysteries, for it is the primal wisdom that the moon enshrines within itself. What the moon is able to reflect from the whole universe forms the sum total of the forces which sustain the animal world of the earth, especially the forces that are connected with the sexual nature of animals; these forces also sustain the animal element in the human being and are connected with his sexual nature in its physical aspect. So the lower nature of the human being is a product of what radiates from the moon, while the highest wisdom once possessed by the earth lies concealed within the moon fortress.

In this way one gradually acquires a knowledge of the 'individuality' of the moon, of what the moon is in reality, whereas all other knowledge is only like information we could glean about a human being from a pasteboard image of him displayed in some exhibition. Such an image would tell us nothing whatever about the human being's individuality. Equally it is not possible for a science that refuses any contact with initiation to know anything about the individuality of the moon.

★   ★   ★

We turn now to Saturn. In earlier times Saturn was regarded as the outermost planet of our system, Uranus and Neptune having been added much later.[47] We will leave them out of consideration now and think of Saturn as a kind of antithesis to the moon.

The nature of Saturn is such that he receives many diverse impulses from the universe but allows none of them to stream back—at all events not to the earth. Saturn too, of course, is irradiated by the sun, but what he reflects of the solar rays has no significance for earthly life. Saturn is an entirely self-engrossed heavenly body in our planetary system, raying his own being into the universe. When we contemplate Saturn, he tells us always what he is. Whereas the moon—contemplated in its external aspect—tells us about everything else in the universe, Saturn tells us nothing at all about the impulses he receives from the universe. He speaks only of himself, tells us only what he himself is. And what he is reveals itself gradually as a kind of memory of the planetary system.

Saturn presents himself to us as the heavenly individuality who has steadfastly participated in whatever has come to pass in our planetary system and has faithfully preserved it in his cosmic memory. He is silent about the cosmic present. He receives the things of the cosmic present into himself and works upon them in his life of spirit and soul. True, the hosts of beings dwelling in Saturn lend their attention to the outer universe, but mutely and silently they receive the happenings in the universe into the realm of soul, and they speak only of past cosmic events. That is why Saturn is like a kaleidoscopic memory of our planetary system. As a faithful informant concerning what has come to pass in the planetary system, he holds its secrets of this kind within himself.

Whereas we would turn to the moon in vain in endeavouring to fathom the mysteries of the universe, whereas we must win the confidence of the moon beings if we are to learn anything from them about cosmic mysteries, this is not necessary with Saturn. With Saturn, all that is necessary is to be open to receive the spiritual. And then, to the eyes of spirit and soul, Saturn becomes a living historian of the planetary system. Nor does he withhold the stories he can tell of what has come to pass in the planetary system. In this respect Saturn is the exact opposite of the moon. Saturn speaks increasingly of the past of the planetary system with such inner warmth and zest that intimate acquaintance with what he says can be dangerous. For the devotion with which he tells of past happenings in the universe arouses in us an overwhelming love for the cosmic past. Saturn is the constant tempter of those who listen to his secrets; he tempts them to give little heed to earthly affairs of today and to immerse themselves in what the earth once was. Above all, Saturn speaks graphically about what the earth was before it became earth, and for this reason he is the planet who makes the past unendingly dear to us. Those who have a particular inclination towards Saturn in earthly existence are people who like to be gazing always into the past, who are opposed to progress, who ever and again want to bring back the past. These indications give some idea of the individuality, the individual character, of Saturn.

★   ★   ★

Jupiter is a planet with a different character. Jupiter is the thinker in our planetary system, and thinking is the activity cultivated by all the beings in his cosmic domain. Creative thoughts received from the universe radiate to us from Jupiter. Jupiter contains, in the form of thoughts, all the formative forces for the various cosmic beings. Whereas Saturn tells of the past, Jupiter gives a living portrayal of what is connected with him in the cosmic present. But what Jupiter reveals to the eye of spirit must be grasped with thoughtful intelligence. If a person does not himself make efforts to develop his capacities of thinking, he cannot, even if he is clairvoyant, approach the mysteries of Jupiter, for they are revealed in the form of thoughts and can be approached only through a genuine activity of thinking. Jupiter is the thinker in our universe.

When efforts to bring clarity of thought to bear upon some weighty problem of existence are unsuccessful because of physical, etheric and especially astral hindrances, the Jupiter beings come to the help of mankind. A person who has tried hard to apply clear thinking to some problem but cannot get to the root of it will find, if he is patient and works inwardly at it, that the Jupiter powers will actually help him during the night. And many a person who has found a better solution for some problem during the night than on the previous day, as though in a dream, would have to admit, if he knew the truth, that it is the Jupiter powers who imbue human thinking with mobility and vigour.

Saturn, then, is the preserver of the memory of our universe; Jupiter is the thinker in our universe. To Jupiter the human being owes all the impulses he is able to receive from the spiritual present in the universe. To Saturn he owes all the impulses of soul and spirit he can receive from the cosmic past.

It was out of a certain intuition that such great veneration was paid to Jupiter in the days of ancient Greece in particular, when the human spirit lived so intensely in the present.

A stimulus to the whole development of the human being is given also through the part played by Jupiter in the cycle of the year. You all know that as far as his apparent movement is concerned Saturn moves slowly, very slowly, round his orbit, taking some 30 years. Jupiter moves faster, taking about 12 years. Because of what he is through this quicker movement, Jupiter is able to satisfy the human being's need for wisdom. And when 'by the clock'—which is in a manner of speaking an expression in the cosmos of the human being's destiny—a certain relationship is established between Jupiter and Saturn, there flash into human destiny those wonderful moments of illumination when many things concerning the past are revealed through thinking.

If we look in history for occasions in the time of the Renaissance—particularly during its last period—when there was a great renewal of ancient impulses, we shall find that this was directly connected with a certain relationship between Jupiter and Saturn.

But, as already said, Jupiter is in a certain respect impenetrable and his revelations remain in the unconscious if a human being does not bring to them clear and active illuminated thoughts of his own. And that is why in ancient times, when active thinking was still at a very early state of development, the progress of humanity was in truth always dependent upon the relation between Jupiter and Saturn. When Jupiter and Saturn together formed a certain constellation, many things were revealed to our ancestors in those days. The modern human being has to depend more upon receiving the memory of Saturn and the wisdom of Jupiter separately in the course of his spiritual development

★   ★   ★

We now come to Mars. It is difficult to find appropriate expressions for these things, but Mars may be called the great 'talker' in the planetary system. Unlike Jupiter, who withholds his wisdom in the form of thoughts, Mars is constantly blurting out to the souls in his sphere whatever in the cosmos is accessible to him—which is not everything. Mars is the most talkative planet in our system, and he is particularly active when human beings talk in sleep or in dreams. Mars has a great longing to be always talking, and whenever some quality in human nature enables him to make a person loquacious, he stimulates this tendency.

Mars does little thinking. He has few thinkers but many talkers in his sphere. The Mars spirits are always on the watch for what arises here or there in the universe and then they talk about it with great zest and fervour. Mars is the planetary individuality who in the course of the evolution of humanity instigates human beings in manifold ways to make statements about the mysteries of the cosmos. Mars has his good and his less good sides—he has his genius and his demon. His genius works in such a way that human beings receive from the universe the impulses for speech; the influence of his demon results in speech being misused in many and various ways. In a certain sense Mars may be called the agitator in our universe. He is always out to persuade, whereas Jupiter wants only to convince.

*   *   *

The planet Venus is again different. In a certain way—how shall I put it?—Venus wards off the universe. She is difficult to approach; she does not want to know anything about the universe. Her attitude is that if she were to expose herself to the external universe, she would lose her virginal nature. She is deeply shocked when any impression from the external universe attempts to approach her. She has no desire for the universe and rejects every would-be partner. It is very difficult to express these things, because the circumstances and conditions have to be described in terms of earthly language. On the other hand, Venus is highly responsive to everything that comes from the earth. The earth is, so to speak, her lover.[48] Whereas the moon reflects the whole surrounding universe, Venus reflects nothing at all of the universe, wants to know nothing of it. But she lovingly reflects whatever comes from the earth. If with the eyes of soul we are able to glimpse the mysteries of Venus, the whole earth with its secrets of the soul life is there before us once again.

The truth is that human beings on earth can do nothing in the secrecy of their souls without it being reflected back again by Venus. Venus gazes deeply into the hearts of human beings, for that is what interests her, that is what she will allow to approach her. Thus the most intimate experiences of earthly life are reflected again from Venus, in a mysterious and wonderful way. In the reflection she transforms everything, just as a dream transforms the happenings of physical existence. Venus transforms the occurrences of earthly life into dream-pictures. In reality, therefore, the whole sphere of Venus is a world of dream. The secrets of human beings in their earthly existence are transformed by Venus into dream-pictures of infinite diversity. She has a very great deal to do with poets, although they are not aware of it.

I said before that Venus wards off the rest of the universe. She does not, however, repel everything in the same way. In her heart, Venus repels what approaches her from the universe but not what comes from the earth. As I said before, she declines every would-be suitor, but for all that she listens attentively to the utterances of Mars. She transforms and illumines her dream-like experiences of earthly things with what is communicated to her from the universe through Mars.

All these things have their physical side as well. Impulses go out from these sources into what is done and what comes into existence in the world. Venus receives into herself everything that comes from the earth and she listens always to Mars—but without any desire that he should be aware of having her attention. And from this process—only of course the sun is there to regulate it—spring the forces which underlie the organs connected with the formation of human speech.

If we want to understand the impulses in the universe connected with the formation of human speech, we must turn our gaze to this strange life that weaves between Venus and Mars. When destiny wills it, the relationship of Venus to Mars is therefore a factor of great significance in the development of the speech or language of a people. A language is deepened, imbued with the quality of soul, when, for example, Venus is square to Mars. On the other hand a language tends to become superficial, poor in qualities of soul, when Venus and Mars are in conjunction, and this in turn has an influence upon the people or nation concerned. Such are the impulses which originate in the universe and then work into the earthly world.

*   *   *

We come next to Mercury. In contrast to the other planets, Mercury is not interested in things of a physical, material nature as such, but in whatever is capable of coordination. Mercury is the domain of the masters of coordinative thinking; Jupiter, the habitation of the masters of wisdom-filled thinking.

When a human being comes down from pre-earthly life into earthly existence, it is the moon impulse that provides the forces for his physical existence. Venus provides the forces for the basic qualities of heart and temperament. But Mercury provides the forces for capacities of intellect and reason, especially of intellect. The masters of the forces of coordinative knowledge and mental activity have their habitation in Mercury.

There is a remarkable connection between these planets and the human being. The moon, which enshrines the beings living in strict seclusion, and reflects only what is first radiated to it from the universe, builds the outer form, the body of the human being. It is therefore by the moon that the forces of heredity are incorporated in his bodily constitution. The moon is the cosmic citadel of those spiritual beings who, in complete seclusion, reflect upon what is transmitted in the stream of heredity flowing from generation to generation by way of the physical.

It is because the moon beings remain so firmly entrenched in their fortress that modern scientists know nothing essential about heredity. From a deeper insight, and in terms of cosmic language, it could be said that when at the present time heredity is discussed in one or another domain of science the latter is 'moon-forsaken' and 'Mars-bewitched'. For science speaks under the influence of the demonic Mars forces and has not even begun to approach the real mysteries of heredity.

Venus and Mercury bring into the human being the karmic element that is connected more with the life of soul and spirit and comes to expression in his qualities of heart and in his temperament. On the other hand, there is a liberating factor in Mars, and especially Jupiter and Saturn when the human being has a right relationship with them. They wrest the human being away from what is determined by destiny and make him into a free being.

Biblical words in a somewhat changed form might be used as follows. Saturn, the faithful custodian of cosmic memory, said: let us make the human being free in the realm of his own memory. As a result, the influence of Saturn was forced into the unconscious; the human being's memory became his own possession and with it he acquired the secure foundation of his personal freedom.

Equally, the inner will impulse contained in acts of free

thinking is due to the grace of Jupiter. It would be in Jupiter's power to rule over and control all the thoughts of human beings. He is the one in whom we find the thoughts of the whole universe if we are capable of gaining access to them. But Jupiter too has withdrawn, leaving human beings to think as free beings.

The element of freedom in speech is due to the fact that Mars too has been gracious. Because Mars was obliged, as it were, to acquiesce in the resolution made by the outer planets and could not exercise any greater coercion, the human being is free, in a certain respect, in the realm of speech too—not entirely, but in a certain respect he is free.

From another point of view, Mars, Jupiter and Saturn may therefore also be called the liberating planets; they give the human being freedom. On the other hand, Venus, Mercury and the moon may be called the destiny-determining planets.

In the midst of all these deeds and impulses of the planetary individualities stands the sun, creating harmony between the liberating and the destiny-determining planets. The sun is the individuality in whom the element of necessity in destiny and the element of human freedom interweave in a most wonderful way. And no one can understand what is contained in the flaming brilliance of the sun unless he is able to behold this interweaving life of destiny and freedom in the light which spreads out into the universe and concentrates again in the solar warmth.

Nor can we grasp anything essential about the nature of the sun as long as we take in only what the physicists know of it. We can grasp the nature of the sun only when we know something of its nature of spirit and soul. In that realm it is the power which imbues with warmth the element of necessity in destiny, resolves destiny into freedom in its flame and, if freedom is misused, condenses it once more into its own active substance. The sun is, as it were, the flame in which freedom becomes a luminous reality in the universe. And at the same time the sun is the substance in which, as condensed ashes, misused freedom is moulded into destiny—until destiny itself can become luminous and pass over into the flame of freedom.

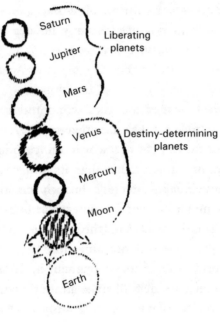

Fig. 5

10. The human being's inner cosmic system

This short extract has been chosen because we are given con-firmation of the traditional teaching which connects the human being's inner organs to the planets Mercury, Venus, sun, Mars, Jupiter and Saturn, thus filling out our knowledge of planetary activity. If it raises further questions, we should bear in mind that we would need to study all the lectures in the course regarding the whole physiology and interconnectedness.

We have, then, something very wonderful in the human blood organism. We have in it an actual, genuine means of expression of the human ego which, on the one hand, faces the external world and, on the other, its own inner life. Just as the human being is directed through his nerve system towards the impressions of this outer world, taking the outer world into himself, as it were, through the nerves by way of the soul, in the same way he comes into direct contact with the outer world through the instrument of his blood, in that the blood receives oxygen from the air through the lungs. We may say, therefore, that in the system of the spleen, liver and gall bladder on the one hand and in the lung system on the other we have two systems which counteract each other. Outer world and inner world, so to speak, have an absolutely direct contact with each other in the human organism by means of the blood, because the blood comes into contact on the one side with the outer air and on the other with the nutritional material that has been deprived of its own nature. One might say that the two cosmic effects come into collision within the human being, like positive and negative electricity. We can very easily picture to ourselves where the organ system is located that is designed to permit the collision of these two systems of cosmic forces to have an effect upon it. The transformed nutritional juices work upwards as far as the heart, inasmuch as the blood which carries them streams through the heart; the oxygen of the air which enters the blood directly from the outer world works inward to the heart, inasmuch as the blood flows through it. In the heart we therefore have that organ in which these two systems into which the human being is interwoven, to which he is attached from two different directions, meet each other. The whole inner organism of the human being is joined to the heart on the one side, and on the other this inner organism itself is connected directly through the heart with the rhythm, the inner vital activity, of the outer world.

It is quite possible that when two such systems collide the direct result of their interaction may be a harmony. The system of the great outside world or macrocosm presses upon us through the fact that it sends the oxygen or the air in general into our inner organism, and the system of our small inner world or microcosm transforms our nourishment. Therefore we might imagine that these systems, because of the fact that the blood streams through the heart, are able in the blood to create a harmonious balance. If this were so, the human being would be yoked to two worlds, so to speak, providing him with his inner equilibrium. Now, we shall see later in the course of these lectures that the connection between the world and the human being is not such that the world leaves us quite passive—that it sends its forces into us in two different ways, while we are simply harnessed to their counteracting influences. No, it is not like that. But rather, as we shall more and more learn to know, the essential thing with regard to the human being is the fact that in the final instance a residue always remains for his own inner activity, and that it is left ultimately to the human being himself to bring about the balance, the inner equilibrium, right into his very organs. We must, therefore, seek within the human organism itself for the balancing of these two world systems, the harmonizing of these two systems of organs. We must realize that the harmonizing of these two organ systems is not already provided through the kind of laws operating outside the human being and the other kind of laws which work only within his own organism, but that this must be evoked through the help of a separate organ system. The human being must establish the harmony within himself. We are not now speaking of conscious activities but of those processes which take place entirely unconsciously within the human organ systems. This balancing of the two systems—the system of spleen, liver, gall bladder on the one hand and the lung system on the other—as they relate to the blood which flows through the heart, indeed happens. It is brought about through the fact that we have the kidney system inserted in the entire human organism and in close relationship with the circulation of the blood.

In the kidney system we have that which harmonizes, as it were, the outer activities resulting from the direct contact of the blood with the air and those other activities proceeding from the inner human organism itself in that the food must first be prepared by being deprived of its own nature. Accordingly, in this kidney system we have a balancing system between the two kinds of organ systems previously characterized; and the organism is in a position by means of this system to dispose of the excess which otherwise would result from the inharmonious interaction of the two other systems.

Over against the entire inner organization, the organs belonging to the digestive apparatus (in which we must include the liver, gall bladder, and spleen), we have placed that system for which these organs primarily develop their preparatory activity, namely the blood system. But also over against this blood system we have placed those organs which work, on the one hand, to counteract a one-sided isolation and, on the other, to create a balance between the inner systems we have mentioned and what presses inward from without. If we think, therefore, of the blood system with its central point, the heart, as placed in the middle of the organism—and we shall see how truly justifiable this is—we have adjoining this system of the blood and heart on the one side the spleen, liver and gall bladder systems and connected with it on the other side the lung and kidney systems. We shall go on to highlight how extremely interesting this connection between the lung system and the kidney system is. If we sketch the systems side by side, we have in them everything belonging to the inner organization of the human being which is related in a special way, and which so presents itself

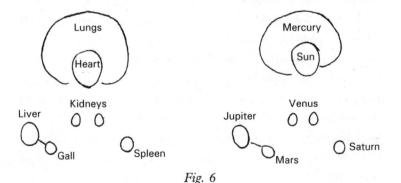

Fig. 6

to us in this relationship that we are obliged to look upon the heart, together with the blood system belonging to it, as by far the most important part. Now, I have already pointed out, and we shall see even more definitely to what an extent such designations as we have described are justified, that from an esoteric perspective the activity of the spleen is characterized as a Saturn activity, that of the liver as a Jupiter activity, and that of the gall bladder as a Mars activity. On the same basis on which these names were chosen for the activities here referred to, esoteric knowledge sees in the heart and the blood system belonging to it something in the human organism which merits the name sun, just as the sun outside merits this name in the planetary system. In the lung system there is contained what the esotericists, according to the same principle, characterize as Mercury, and in the kidney system that which merits the name Venus. Thus by means of these names we have pointed out in these systems of the human organism, even if at the present moment we will not seek to justify the names, something like an inner cosmic system. We have, moreover, supplemented this inner cosmic system in that we have placed ourselves in a position to observe the relationship arising from the very nature of the human being as holding good for the two other organ systems which have a certain connection with the blood system. Only when we observe these things in such a way do we present something complete in respect of what we may call the real inner human world. In the following lectures I shall have occasion to show you that esotericists have real reasons for conceiving the relationship of the sun to Mercury and Venus as being similar to that which we must think of as existing between the heart and lungs and kidneys in the human organism.

We see, therefore, that in the instrument of our ego our blood system, which expresses its rhythm in the heart, something is present that is determined to a certain extent in its entire formation, its inner nature and quality of being, by the human being's inner cosmic system—something that must first be embedded in the inner cosmic system of the human being before it can live as it actually does live. We have in the human blood system, as I have often stated, the physical instrument of our ego. Indeed, we know that our ego as constituted is only possible by reason of the fact that it is built up on the foundation of a physical body, an etheric body and an astral body. An ego free to fly about in the world by itself, as a human ego, is unthinkable. A human ego within this world, which is the world that for the moment concerns us, presupposes as its basis an astral body, an etheric body and a physical body.

11. The planetary spheres and life between death and rebirth

But how is it really that the planets have an influence on human beings if it is not a matter of 'sending down rays' (apart from their forces when organs are still developing)? It is because in the time spent between incarnations, when we are in the spiritual world, our future karma is prepared together with spiritual beings. This mighty activity is mainly carried out during the periods spent in the planetary spheres.

Other surprising questions are raised here too. Steiner speaks of 'Mars dwellers' for example. This is because the spheres are not empty of beings, but it should not be assumed that physical beings like ourselves dwell on Mars and travel here in UFOs. People claiming to have visits from Mars or Venus inhabitants—the 'wanderers'—are much more likely to be having a supersensory experience, enhanced sometimes perhaps by magnetic forces in some way, so as to appear physically real. Another remarkable piece of research that is unknown to the wider astrological world is that Mars is evolving too and has undergone a change, a deed wrought by Buddha, so that its potential is no longer aggressive and warlike (though this will also manifest for a long time to come if it is what people choose to absorb). If we are to understand this rightly it will mean learning to interpret horoscopes in a new way. For example we can see in the case of Gandhi's horoscope how the transformed Mars forces worked as a signature by observing that Mars together with Venus and Mercury were rising at his birth in the Mars-governed sign of Scorpio.

The first period after a human being's death is filled with experiences connected in some way with his recent life on earth. He is emerging from, growing away from, his last earthly life, and during the first period after death the emotions, passions and feelings that affected his astral body all continue to exist. Because during physical incarnation the human being is conscious of these feelings only when he is actually within his physical body, it is natural that his experiences of all these forces in the astral body is essentially different when he is passing through the region of existence between death and a new birth. In normal cases, although there are many exceptions, a sense of deprivation is present during the first period after death. This is due to the fact that the human being must live through the experiences in his astral body without having a physical body at his disposal. He still longs for his physical body, and in normal cases this longing holds him back in the sphere of the earth for a longer or shorter period. Life in kamaloka takes its course in the sphere between the earth and the orbit of the moon, but experiences in kamaloka that are of essential significance take place in a realm nearer the earth than, let us say, the orbit of the moon.

Souls who have unfolded only few feelings and sentiments transcending the affairs of earthly life remain bound to the earth sphere by their own cravings for a considerable time. Even outwardly it is easy to understand that a human being who for a whole lifetime has cultivated only such feelings as can be satisfied by means of bodily organs and earthly conditions can but remain bound to the earth sphere for a certain time. Impulses and desires quite different from those ordinarily imagined can also cause a soul to remain bound to the earth sphere. Ambitious people, for instance, who cultivate an inordinate longing for certain things within earthly conditions and who depend on the appreciation of their fellow human beings thereby develop an emotional disturbance in their astral body that will result in their being bound to the earth sphere for a longer time after death. There are many reasons for which human souls are held back in the earth sphere. By far the greater majority of communications from the spirit world made by mediums stem from such souls and consist essentially of what they are striving to cast off.

Although the motives binding these souls to the earth are mostly ignoble, it need not invariably be so. It may also be due to anxiety for those who have been left behind on earth. Concern for friends, relatives and children may also act as a kind of gravity that holds souls back in the earth sphere. It is important to pay attention to this because by taking it into account we can also help the dead. If, for instance, we realize that the departed soul feels anxiety for a living person—and much can come to our knowledge in this respect—it will help the dead person in his further development to relieve him of this anxiety. We ease the life of someone who has died by relieving him, for example, of anxiety about a child whom he has left behind unprovided for. By doing something for the child, we relieve the dead person of anxiety, and this is a true service of love. Let us picture such a situation. The dead person has not available the means to rid himself of anxiety. From his realm he may be unable to do anything that would ease the circumstances of a child, a relative or a friend. He is often condemned—and in many cases this weighs heavily upon the seer—to bear the anxiety until the situation of the one left behind improves of itself or by circumstances. Therefore, if we do something to better the situation we will have performed a real deed of love for the dead one.

It has frequently been observed that a person who had planned to do something definite in life died and then continued to cling to the plan after his death. We help him if we ourselves attempt to do what he would have liked to do. These situations are not difficult to grasp. We should take account of them because they tally with clairvoyant observation.

There are many other facts that may keep a soul in the etheric sphere of the earth. Eventually he grows beyond this sphere. This process has already partly been described. Our concepts must be recast if we wish to gain an understanding of the life between death and rebirth. It is not really incongruous to speak about the dead in words taken from the conditions of earthly existence because our language is adapted to these conditions. Although what can be expressed in words about life after death tallies only in a pictorial sense, it need not necessarily be incorrect.

Descriptions are never quite accurate that convey the idea that the dead are confined to a definite place like a being who is living in a physical body. What is experienced both after death and in initiation is that one is emerging from the body and one's whole soul being is expanding. When we follow a soul who has reached the moon sphere as we call it, the 'body' denotes the expansion of the range of experience. In actual fact the human being grows, in a spiritual sense, to gigantic dimensions. He grows out into the spheres, but the spheres of the dead are not separate from each other as in the case of human beings on earth. They are spatially intermingled. A sense of separateness arises because consciousness is separate. Beings may be completely intermingled without knowing anything of one another.

The feeling of either isolation or community after death of

which I spoke during my last visit is connected with the interrelationships of consciousness. It is not as if a dead person were on some isolated island in a spatial sense. He pervades the other being of whose existence he is totally unaware although they occupy the same space.

Let us now consider what comes about mainly when the period of kamaloka is over. When an individual enters upon his devachanic existence after passing through the moon sphere, kamaloka is not yet entirely at an end. This does not preclude the fact that it is within the moon sphere that adjustments take place that are of significance not only as kamaloka experiences, but also for the later life of the individual when he again enters existence through birth. We can characterize in the following way what is added to the kamaloka experiences. A human being may be so active in life that he brings all his talents to expression. But there are many human beings of whom we have to say, when we observe them with the eyes of the soul, that according to their faculties and talents they could have achieved in life something quite different from what they have in fact achieved. Such people have lagged behind their talents.

Something else comes into consideration. There are people who nurture a great number of intentions in the course of their life. It need not be a question of talent, but of intentions connected either with trivial or important aims. How much in life merely remains at the stage of intention without being fulfilled!

There are things in this category that need not be considered blameworthy. In order to show how significant such things may be I will mention an instance already known to some friends. Goethe embarked in his *Pandora* upon a poetical work and at a certain point he came to a standstill. I once explained what happened to Goethe when writing *Pandora* in the following way. The very greatness that had conceived the plan of the poem prevented him from completing the work. He was incapable of unfolding the power whereby the plan could have turned into reality. It was not because of shortcomings but in a sense because of his greatness that Goethe was prevented from completing *Pandora*. This is the case with some of his other works, too. He left them unfinished. The fragment of *Pandora* shows that Goethe made such considerable artistic demands upon himself that his powers, even in respect of the outer form of the poem, were simply not able to carry out the entire mighty plan with the same ease as in the fragment with which he was successful. This is obviously an example of an unfulfilled intention.

Therefore, on the one hand, a person may lag behind his talents owing to laziness or to defects in character or intellect, but the other possibility is that he may not be able to carry out his intentions in small or important matters. Now there is something great in a poet who does not complete a work such as *Pandora*, but every imperfection in the human being is inscribed by him into the Akasha Chronicle in the moon sphere, and thus an abundance of shortcomings and imperfections come before the eye of the seer in the realm between earth and moon. Human imperfections, be they noble or not, are faithfully recorded there. Instances can be found in which, through physical health, through a bodily constitution providing a good foundation for intellectual gifts, a person would have been capable of achieving certain things but failed to do so. What he could have become but had not become when he passed through the gate of death—this is inscribed in the Akasha Chronicle.

Do not imagine that the end of *Pandora* is in some way inscribed in the moon sphere. What is inscribed has to do with Goethe's astral body, namely that he had conceived a great, far-reaching plan and only fulfilled a part of it. All such things, including trivial matters, are inscribed between the spheres of earth and moon. A person who forms a resolution but has not carried it out before his death inscribes the fact of non-fulfilment in this sphere. A fairly accurate characterization can be given of what is disclosed to the eye of seership in this realm. A promise that has not been kept, for example, is not inscribed until later, actually not until the Mercury sphere is reached. An unfulfilled resolution, however, is inscribed in the moon sphere. Anything that affects not only ourselves but also others is not immediately inscribed in the moon sphere, but only later. Anything that affects us as individuals, that keeps us behind our proper stage of evolution and thus denotes imperfection in our personal development is inscribed in the moon sphere.

It is important to realize that our imperfections, especially those that need not have been inevitable, are inscribed in the moon sphere.

It should not be thought that in all circumstances such an inscription is a dreadful thing. In a certain sense it can be of the greatest value and significance. We will speak in a moment of the meaning and purpose of these inscriptions in the Akasha Chronicle. First it must be emphasized that as the person expands into other spheres all his imperfections are there inscribed. He expands from the moon sphere into the Mercury sphere; I am speaking entirely from the aspect of esotericism, not from that of ordinary astronomy. Something is inscribed by him in all the spheres, in the Mercury sphere, the Venus sphere, the sun sphere, the Mars sphere, the Jupiter sphere, the Saturn sphere and even beyond.

Most inscriptions, however, are made within the sun sphere, for as we heard in the last lecture, outside the sun sphere the human being mainly has to adjust matters that are not just left to his own individual discretion.

Thus after having cast away more or less completely what still draws him to the earth, the human being journeys through the planetary spheres and even beyond them. The contact thus established with the corresponding forces provides what he needs in his evolution between death and a new birth. When I spoke in the last lecture of the human being coming into contact with the higher hierarchies and receiving the gifts they bestow, that was the same as saying that his being expands into the cosmos. When the expansion has been completed he contracts again until he has become minute enough to unite as a spirit-seed with what comes from the parents. This is indeed a wonderful mystery. When the human being passes through the gate of death he himself becomes an ever-expanding sphere. His potentialities of soul and spirit expand. He becomes a gigantic being and then again contracts. What we have within us has in fact contracted from the planetary universe. Quite literally we bear within us what we have lived through in a planetary world.

When I was here last I said certain things about the passage through the Mercury sphere, the Venus sphere and the sun sphere. Our being expands and becomes larger and larger. This is not an easy concept but that is what actually happens. It is only on earth that we consider ourselves limited within the boundary of our skin. After death we expand into the infinite spaces, growing ever larger. When we have reached the end of the kamaloka period we literally extend to the orbit of the moon around the earth. In the language of esotericism we become moon dwellers. Our being has expanded to such an extent that its outer boundary coincides with the circle described by the moon around the earth. Today I cannot go into the relative positions of the planets. An explanation of what does not apparently agree with orthodox astronomy can be found in the Düsseldorf lectures, *Spiritual Hierarchies and the Physical World: Reality and Illusion.*[49]

Thus we grow farther out into cosmic space, into the whole planetary system, though first into what the occultist calls the Mercury sphere. That is to say, after the kamaloka period we become Mercury dwellers. We truly feel that we are inhabiting cosmic space. Just as during our physical existence we feel ourselves to be earth dwellers, so then we feel ourselves to be Mercury dwellers. I cannot describe the details now, but the following conscious experience is present. We are not now enclosed in such a small fraction of space as during our earthly existence but the wide sphere bounded by the orbit of Mercury is within our being. How we live through this period also depends upon how we have prepared ourselves on earth—on the forces we have imbibed on earth in order to grow into the right or wrong relationship to the Mercury sphere.

In order to understand these facts we can compare two or more people by means of occult research but we will take two. For instance, let us consider a human being who passed through the gate of death with an immoral attitude and one who passed through the gate of death with a moral attitude of soul. A considerable difference is perceptible and it becomes apparent when we consider the relationship of one person to another after death. For the human being with a moral attitude of soul the pictures are also present, enveloping the soul, but he can have a certain degree of communion everywhere with other human beings. This is due to his moral attitude. The human being with an immoral attitude of soul becomes a kind of hermit in the spiritual world. For example, he knows that another human being is also in the spiritual world. He knows that he is together with him but he is unable to emerge from the prison of his cloud of imaginations and approach him. Morality makes us into social beings in the spiritual world, into beings who can have contact with others. Lack of morality makes us into hermits in the spiritual world and transports us into solitude. This is an important causal connection between what lives in our souls here on earth and what occurs between death and rebirth.

This is true also of the further course of events. At a later period, after having passed through the Mercury sphere in an esoteric sense, we live through the Venus sphere, we feel ourselves as Venus dwellers. There between Mercury and Venus, where our cloud of images is illuminated from without, the beings of the higher hierarchies are able to approach the human being. Now again it depends on whether we have prepared ourselves in the right manner to be received as social spirits into the ranks of the hierarchies and to have communion with them, or whether we are compelled to pass them by as hermits. Whether we are social or lonely spirits depends upon still another factor. Whereas in the previous sphere we can be sociable only if this has been prepared on earth as a result of morality, in the Venus sphere the power that leads us into community, into a kind of social life, is due to our religious attitude on earth. We most certainly condemn ourselves to become hermits in the Venus sphere if we have failed to develop religious feelings during earthly life, feelings of union with the infinite, with the divine.

Esoteric investigation observes that as a result of an atheistic tendency in the soul, of rejecting the connection of our finite with our infinite nature, the human being locks himself up within his own prison. It is a fact that the adherents of the Monistic Union,[50] with its creed that does not promote a truly religious attitude, are preparing themselves for a condition in which they will no longer be able to form any Monistic Union, but will be relegated each to his own separate prison!

This is not meant to be a principle on which to base judgements. It is a fact that presents itself to esoteric observation as the consequence of a religious or irreligious attitude of soul during earthly life. Many different religions have been established on the earth in the course of evolution, all of them emanating essentially from a common source. Their founders have had to reckon with the temperament of the different peoples, with the climate and with other factors to which the religions had to be adjusted. It is therefore in the nature of things that souls did not come into this Venus sphere with a common religious consciousness, but with one born of their particular creed.

Definite feelings for the spiritual that are coloured by this or that religious creed mean that in the Venus sphere a human being has community only with those of like feelings who shared the same creed during earthly life. In the Venus sphere individuals are separated according to their particular creeds. On the earth they were divided into races according to external characteristics. Although the configuration of groups in the Venus sphere corresponds in general to the groupings of people here on earth because racial connections are related to religious creeds, the groupings do not quite correspond because there they are brought together according to their understanding of a particular creed. As a result of experience connected with a particular creed, souls enclose themselves within certain boundaries. In the Mercury sphere the human being has, above all, understanding for those with whom he was connected on earth. If he had a moral attitude of soul, he will have real interaction in the Mercury sphere with those to whom he was related during his earthly life. In the Venus sphere he is taken up into one of the great religious communities to which he belonged during his earthly existence by virtue of his constitution of soul.

The next sphere is the sun sphere in which we feel ourselves as sun dwellers for a definite period between death and rebirth. During this period we learn to know the nature of the sun, which is quite different from the description of astronomy today. Here again it is a question of living rightly into the sun sphere. We now have the outstanding experience, and it arises in the soul like an elemental power, that all differentiations between human souls must cease. In the Mercury sphere we are more or less limited to the circle of those with whom we were related on earth. In the Venus sphere we feel at home with those who had similar religious experiences to ours on earth and we still find satisfaction only among these communities. But the soul is conscious of deep loneliness in the sun sphere if it has no understanding for the souls entering this sphere, as is the case with Felix Balde[51] for instance. Now in ancient times conditions were such that in the Venus sphere souls were to be found in the provinces of the several religions, finding and giving understanding in them. Because all religions have sprung from a common source, when the human being entered the sun sphere he had in him so much of the old common inheritance that he could come near to all the other souls in the sun sphere and be together with them, to understand them, to be a social spirit among them.

In the more ancient periods of human evolution, souls could not do much of themselves to satisfy the longing that arose there. Because without human intervention a common human nucleus was present in humankind, it was possible for souls to have interaction with others belonging to different creeds. In ancient Brahmanism, in the Chinese and other religions of the earth, there was so much of the common kernel of religion that souls in the sun sphere found themselves in that primal home, the source of all religious life. This changed in the middle period of the earth. Connection with the primal source of the religions was lost and can only be found again through esoteric knowledge. So in the present cycle of evolution the human being must also prepare himself for entering the sun sphere while still on earth because community does not arise there of itself. The Mystery of Golgotha, of Christianity, is also important in this respect. Because of the latter, human beings in the present cycle of evolution can prepare themselves on earth for universal community to be achieved in the sun sphere. For this purpose the sun spirit, the Christ, had to come down to earth. Since his coming, it has been possible for souls on the earth to find the way to universal community in the sun sphere between death and rebirth.

Today I wish to speak about certain aspects of the passage through the Mars sphere. When a human being passes from the sun sphere into the Mars sphere, the conditions of existence into which he enters are quite different in our present age from what they were a comparatively short time ago. To the eyes of the seer it is quite evident that there was good reason for the statements, based on the clairvoyance once possessed by humanity, about the various bodies composing the planetary system. It was entirely in keeping with the facts that Mars was considered to be the member of our planetary system connected with all warlike, aggressive elements in the evolution of humanity. The fantastic theories advanced by physical astronomy today about a possible form of life on Mars are without foundation. The nature of the beings whom we might call 'Mars people' if we wish to use such an expression, is altogether different from that of the people on earth, and no comparison is possible. Until the seventeenth century the character of the Mars beings had invariably been one of warlike aggressiveness.

Belligerency, if one may use this word, was an inherent quality of the Mars 'culture'. The basis of it was formed by the rivalries and clashes between souls perpetually battling with each other. As an individual was passing through the Mars sphere between death and rebirth, he came into contact with these forces of aggression and they made their way into his soul. If when he was born again his innate tendencies made him specially able to develop and give expression to these forces, it was to be attributed to his passage through the Mars sphere.

This subject is full of complications. On the earth we live among the beings of the three kingdoms of nature, and among human beings. By various means we come into contact with the souls who in their life after death still retain some connection with the earth but we also encounter beings who are utterly foreign to the earth. The more an initiate is able to widen his vision, the more souls are found who are strangers on the earth, and the more it is realized that wanderers are passing through the earth sphere. They are beings who are not connected with earthly life in the normal way.

This is no different for us as human beings on earth than it is for the moon dwellers through whose sphere of life we also pass between death and a new birth. When we are passing through the Mars sphere, for example, we are ghosts, spectres, for the Mars dwellers. We pass through their sphere as strangers, as alien beings. But the Mars beings, too, at a certain stage of their existence, are condemned to pass through our earth sphere and a person who possesses certain initiate faculties encounters them when conditions are favourable.

Beings of our planetary system are continually streaming past each other. While we are living on earth, often imagining that we are surrounded only by the beings of the different kingdoms of nature, there are itinerants from all the other planets in our environment. During a certain period between death and a new birth we, too, are itinerants among the other planetary 'people' if one might speak in this way. We have to develop in our lives on earth the essentials of our particular mission in the present epoch of cosmic existence. Other beings are allotted to the other planetary worlds, and between death and rebirth we must contact these worlds, too. Therefore, when reference is made to one region or another of life in Devachan, it is actually the case, although it is not expressly stated, that the events are taking place in some sphere of our planetary system. This should be borne in mind. Thus at a certain time in life between death and a new birth we pass through the Mars sphere.

Just as the process of Earth evolution is a process of descent until the time of the Mystery of Golgotha, and of ascent from then onwards, so also do the other planets undergo an evolution in their own way. From AD 33, the date is approximately correct, the earth entered upon an ascending process of evolution. That year was the pivotal point in the earth's evolution. On Mars the pivotal point was at the beginning of the seventeenth century. Until then, the evolution of conditions on Mars had been a process of descent and from that time onwards a process of ascent has occurred because an event of the greatest significance for that planet then took place.

In connection with Earth evolution, we know of the remarkable personage: Gautama Buddha. He was a Bodhisattva until in the twenty-ninth year of his life he rose to the rank of Buddhahood and was then destined never to be incarnated again in a physical body on earth. From other lectures you will have heard, however, that later on the Buddha still worked into the earth sphere from the spiritual world. He sent his forces into the astral body of the Jesus child of the Gospel of St Luke.[52] But in another way, too, he influenced earthly life without incarnating into a physical body. In the seventh and eighth centuries there was a mystery school in the south-east of Europe for those who at that time were endowed with some degree of seership. The teachers in that school were not only individualities in physical incarnation but there were also those who work from spiritual heights only as far as the etheric body. It is possible for more highly developed human beings to receive instruction from individualities who no longer, or never, descend into a physical body. The Buddha himself was a teacher in the mystery school. Among his pupils at that time was the personality who was born later on in his next incarnation as Francis of Assisi.[53] Many of the qualities so impressively displayed in that later life are to be traced to the fact that Francis of Assisi had been a pupil of the Buddha.

Here we see how the Buddha continued to work from

spiritual heights into the earth sphere after the Mystery of Golgotha, and how he was connected with the life of the human being between birth and death.

Then, in the seventeenth century, the Buddha withdrew from earthly existence and accomplished for Mars a deed that, although not of the magnitude of the Mystery of Golgotha, nevertheless resembled it and corresponded on Mars to the Mystery of Golgotha on earth. At the beginning of the seventeenth century the Buddha became the redeemer, the saviour of Mars. He was the individuality whose mission it was to inculcate peace and harmony into the aggressive nature of Mars. Since then the Buddha impulse is to be found on Mars as the Christ impulse is to be found on the earth since the Mystery of Golgotha.

The destiny of the Buddha on Mars was not death as in the Mystery of Golgotha. Yet in a certain respect it, too, was a kind of crucifixion inasmuch as this wonderful individuality, who in keeping with his life on earth radiated universal peace and love, was transferred into the midst of what was completely alien to him, into the aggressive, warlike element on Mars. It was Buddha's mission to exercise a pacifying influence on Mars. For the gaze of seership there is something tremendously impressive in the picture of two collateral events. The Buddha had risen to the highest point attainable in his earthly existence, to the rank of Buddhahood, and had lived on earth as the Buddha for 50 years. Then in his eightieth year, on 13 October 483 BC, on a glorious moonlit night, he breathed out his being into the silvery radiance glimmering over the earth. This event, which even outwardly seems to be a manifestation of the breath of peace emanating from the Buddha, bears witness to the fact that he had attained the zenith of development within his earthly existence. It is deeply impressive to contemplate this wonderful happening in connection with that moment at the beginning of the seventeenth century when, with all his abounding powers of peace and love, the Buddha went to Mars in order that those powers might stream from him into the aggressiveness prevailing there to gradually inaugurate the process of Mars' ascending evolution.

When a soul passed through the Mars sphere in times before the Buddha Mystery, it was endowed primarily with forces of aggressiveness. Since the Buddha Mystery a soul undergoes essentially different experiences if it has the disposition to gain something from the Mars forces. To avoid any misunderstanding it must be emphasized that as little as the whole earth today is already Christianized, as little has Mars become entirely a planet of peace. That process will still take a long time so that if a soul has any aptitude for receiving elements of aggressiveness there is still ample opportunity for it. Nevertheless, we must not lose sight, spiritually, of the event of which we have spoken. The more deeply the earth enters into a phase of materialism, the less will anyone who really understands the evolutionary process admit that it would be natural for a human being in his life between birth and death to follow Buddha in the way that men followed him in pre-Christian times. The development of natures such as that of Francis of Assisi will gradually become less and less possible on earth, less and less suitable for external civilization. Nevertheless, between death and rebirth the soul is able to pass through this experience. Grotesque as it may seem, yet it corresponds to the facts, for a certain period between death and a new birth, during the passage through the Mars sphere, every human soul has the opportunity of being a Franciscan or a Buddhist and of receiving all the forces that can flow from feeling and experience of this kind. The passage through the Mars sphere can therefore be of great importance for the human soul. The human being, however, inscribes his perfections and imperfections into whatever sphere he enters according to their affinity with the characteristic qualities of that sphere.

Between death and rebirth our perfections and imperfections are faithfully recorded in the Akasha Chronicle. Certain attributes are inscribed in the moon sphere, others in the Venus sphere, others in the Mars sphere, others in the Mercury sphere, others in the Jupiter sphere, and so on. When we are returning to an incarnation in a physical body and our being is slowly contracting, we encounter everything that was inscribed on the outward journey. In this way our karma is prepared. On the path of return we can inscribe into our own being the record of an imperfection we ourselves first inscribed into the Akasha Chronicle. Then we arrive on the earth. Because there is within us everything we inscribed into our being on the return journey, and we are obliged to inscribe a great deal even if not everything, because of this our karma unfolds. Up above, however, everything still remains inscribed.

Now these inscriptions work together in a remarkable way. They are engraved into the spheres, into the moon sphere, Venus sphere, and so on. These spheres are involved in certain movements so that the following may happen. Let us say that a human being has inscribed one of his imperfections into the moon sphere. While passing through the Mars sphere he has inscribed there a quality of his character through the fact that he acquired in that sphere a certain element of aggressiveness that was not previously in him. Now on the return journey he passes through the Mars sphere again and comes back to the earth. He lives on the earth and has received into his karma what he has inscribed in the Mars sphere but at the same time it stands recorded above him. Up there is Mars, in a certain relationship to the moon. (The outer planets indicate the relative positions of the spheres.) Because Mars stands in a certain relationship to the moon, the inscription of the aggressive element and the human being's imperfections are, as it were, in the same constellation. The consequence is that when the one planet stands behind the other they work in conjunction. This is the time when the individual in question will tackle his imperfection with the aggressive quality acquired from Mars. So the position of the planets really does indicate what the human being himself has first inscribed into these spheres.

When in astrology we ascertain the positions of the planets and also their relative positions to those of the fixed stars, this gives some indication of what we ourselves have inscribed. The outer planets are in this case a less important factor. What actually has an effect upon us is what we ourselves have inscribed in the several spheres. Here is the real reason why the planetary constellations have an effect upon the human being's nature. It is because he actually passes through the several planetary spheres. When the moon stands in a certain relationship to Mars and to some fixed star, this constellation works as a whole. That is to say, the Mars quality, moon and fixed star work in conjunction upon the human being and bring about what this combined influence is able to achieve.

So it is really the moral inheritance deposited by us between death and rebirth that appears again in a new life as a stellar constellation in our karma. That is the deeper basis of the connection between the stellar constellation and the human being's karma. Thus if we study the life of a human being between death and a new birth we perceive how significantly he is connected with the whole cosmos.

An element of necessity enters into a human being's connection with the realms lying beyond the sun sphere. Let us consider the Saturn sphere in particular. If during his present earth life a person has made efforts to master the concepts of spiritual science, the passage through the Saturn sphere is of special significance for his next life. It is in this sphere that the conditions are created that enable him to transmute the forces acquired through the knowledge of spiritual science or anthroposophy into forces that elaborate his bodily constitution in such a way that in his coming life he has a natural inclination towards the spiritual. A person may grow up today and be educated as a materialist, Protestant or Catholic. Spiritual science approaches him. He is receptive to it and does not reject it. He inwardly accepts it. He now passes through the gate of death. He enters the Saturn sphere. In passing through it, he absorbs the forces that make him in his next life a spiritual person, who shows even as a child an inclination to the spiritual.

It is the function of every sphere through which we pass between death and rebirth to transform what our souls have assimilated during an incarnation into forces that can then become bodily forces and endow us with certain faculties. Yesterday I could only go as far as is possible in a public lecture when I said that the true Christian impulses were already in Raphael[54] when he was born. This must not be taken to imply that Raphael brought with him some definite Christian concepts or ideas. I said impulses, not concepts. What has been taken into the conceptual life in one incarnation is united with the human being in quite a different form. It appears as impulses or forces. The power that enabled Raphael to create those delicate, wonderful figures of Christianity in his paintings came from his earlier incarnations. We are justified in speaking of him as a 'born Christian'. Most of you know that Raphael had been incarnated previously as John the Baptist, and it was then that the impulses that appeared in the Raphael existence as inborn Christian impulses had penetrated into his soul.

It must always be emphasized that conjectures and comparisons may lead far off the mark when speaking about successive incarnations. To the eyes of seership they present themselves in such a way that in most cases one would not take one life to be the cause of the next. In order that something assimilated in the life of the soul in one incarnation can unfold forces in the next incarnation that work upon the bodily foundation of talents, we must pass through the period from death to rebirth. On earth and with terrestrial forces it is impossible to transform what our souls have experienced in earthly life into forces capable of working upon the bodily constitution itself. The human being in his totality is not an earth being, and his physical form would have a grotesque appearance according to modern ideas if only those forces present in the earth sphere could be applied to his bodily development.

When an individual comes into existence through birth he must bear within him the forces of the cosmos, and these forces must continue to work within him if he is to assume human form. Forces that build up and give shape to such a form cannot be found within the earth sphere. This must be borne in mind. Thus in what he is the human being bears the image of the cosmos in himself, not merely that of the earth. It is a sin against the true nature of the human being to trace his source and origin to earthly forces, and to study only what can be observed externally in the kingdoms of the earth through natural science. Nor should we ignore the fact that everything the human being receives from the earth is dominated by what he brings with him from those supra-earthly spheres through which he passes between death and rebirth. Within these several spheres he becomes a servant of one or the other of the higher hierarchies.

What is inscribed in the Akasha Chronicle between the earth and the moon is of special importance because it is there that, among other things, all imperfections are recorded. It should be realized that these imperfections are inscribed from the point of view that every record there is of significance for the individual's own evolution, either fur-thering or hindering his progress. Because it is there inscribed in the Akasha Chronicle between earth and moon, it also becomes significant for the evolution of the earth as a whole. The imperfections of really great people are also recorded in that sphere. One example of tremendous interest for clairvoyant observation is Leonardo da Vinci.[55] He is a spirit of greatness and universality equalled by few others on earth, but compared with what he intended, his actual achievements in the external world in many respects remained incomplete. As a matter of fact, no person of similar eminence left as much uncompleted as Leonardo da Vinci. The consequence of this was that a colossal amount was inscribed by him in the moon sphere, so much indeed that one is often bound to exclaim, 'How could all that is inscribed there possibly have reached perfection on the earth!'

At this point I want to tell you of something that seemed to me quite significant when I was studying Leonardo da Vinci. I was to give a lecture about him in Berlin and a particular observation made in connection with him seemed to be extremely important. It fills one with sadness today to see on the wall of the Church of Santa Maria delle Grazie in Milan the rapidly disappearing colours that now convey no more than a faint shadow of what the picture once was. If we remember that Leonardo took 16 years to paint this picture, and think of how he painted it, we gain a definite impression. It is known that he would often go away for a long time. Then he would return to the picture, sit in front of it for many hours, make a few strokes with the brush and go off again. It is also known that on many occasions he felt unable to express what he wished in the painting and suffered terrible fits of depression on this account. Now it happened that a new prior was appointed to the monastery at a time when Leonardo had already been working at the picture for many years. This prior was a pedantic and strict disciplinarian with little understanding of art. He asked impatiently why the painter could not finish the picture, reproached him for it and also complained to Duke Ludovico. The Duke repeated the complaint to Leonardo and he answered, 'I do not know whether I shall ever be able to complete this picture. I have prototypes in life for all the figures except those of Judas and Christ. For them I have no models, although in the case of Judas if no model turns up I can always take the prior. But for the Christ I have no prototype.' But I digress.

What I want to say is that when one looks today at the figure of Judas in the painting that has almost completely faded, a shadow can be seen on this figure, a shadow that cannot be explained in any way, either by the instreaming light or by anything else. Esoteric research finds that the painting was never as Leonardo da Vinci really wanted it to be. With the exception of the figures of Judas and the Christ he wanted to portray everything through light and shadow, but Judas was to be portrayed in such a way as to give the impression that darkness dominated his countenance from within. This was not intended to be conveyed by external contrasts of light and shadows. In the figure of Christ the impression was to be that the light on his countenance was shining from within, radiating outwards from within. But at this point disharmony beset Leonardo's inner life, and the effect he desired was never produced.

This affords a clue when one is observing the many remaining inscriptions made by Leonardo in the moon sphere. It is an example of something that could not be brought to fulfilment in the earth sphere.

When we look at the period following that of Leonardo da Vinci, we find that Leonardo continued to work through a number of those who lived after him. Even externally there can be found in Leonardo's writings things that later on were demonstrated by scientists and also by artists. In fact, the whole subsequent period was under his influence. We then see that the inscribed imperfections worked as inspirations into the souls of Leonardo's successors, into the souls of the people who lived after him.

The imperfections of an earlier epoch are more important for the following epoch than its perfections. The perfections are there to be studied, but what has been elaborated to a certain degree of perfection on the earth has, as it were, reached an end, has come to a conclusion in evolution. What has not been perfected is the seed of the following divine evolutionary process. Here we come to a remarkable, magnificent paradox. The greatest blessing for a subsequent period is the fruitful imperfection, the fruitful, justifiable imperfection of an earlier period. What has been perfected in an earlier epoch is there to be enjoyed. Imperfection, however, imperfection originating in great men and women whose influences have remained for posterity, helps to promote creative activity in the following period. Hence there is obviously tremendous wisdom in the fact that imperfections remain in the vicinity of the earth, inscribed in the records of the Akasha Chronicle between earth and moon.

This brings us to the point where we can begin to understand the principle that perfection signifies the end of evolution, of a stream of evolution in the different epochs; imperfection may mean the beginning of an evolutionary stream. Human beings should actually be thankful to the gods for imperfection in this sense.

What is the purpose of studies such as are contained in this lecture? The purpose is to make the human being's connection with the macrocosm more and more comprehensible, to show how human beings bear the macrocosm compressed within them and also how they can relate to their spiritual environment. Realization of what these things mean can then be transformed into a feeling that pervades the human being in such a way that he combines with this knowledge a concept of his dignity that does not make him arrogant, but fills him with a sense of responsibility, prompts him to believe not that he may squander his powers, but that he must use them.

It must, of course, be emphasized that there is no benefit in saying, 'I had better leave imperfect such faculties as I possess.' Nothing whatever would be gained by such an attitude! If a person were deliberately to ignore his imperfections, he would, it is true, inscribe them as described, but they would have no light nor would they be capable of having any effect. Only those imperfections that are inscribed because they were due to necessity and not the result of laziness can work in the way that has been described.

12. The spiritual preparation of the human body between death and a new birth

Here we find a picture of how the mighty panorama of events and deeds in the spiritual world is actually woven together and condensed to form a person's astral and etheric bodies. In the case of the spiritual seed of the physical body, we saw in the earlier two lectures how this is formed from the zodiacal constellations as a human archetype. We can be reminded of the kabbalistic idea of Adam Kadmon or of the Giant Ymir in the Norse tradition. Then the etheric body is drawn from the cosmic life forces and, together with the ego—the reincarnating individuality—and the astral or 'starry' body prepared in planetary spheres as described in the last lecture, joins the 'spirit seed' sent on ahead to reserve, as it were, the fertilized ovum. We are reminded that our imperfections are also 'collected' on this descent and woven into the subtle bodies in the moon sphere before the final uniting. With the etheric body comes the means for introducing specific individuality into the physical body for each human being, and also, though not mentioned here, the timing for future events of karmic importance to occur on earth (the etheric body is sometimes called the time-body).

This is the great mystery, that the human being's heavenly occupation consists in weaving together with the spirits of the higher hierarchies the great spiritual seed of the future terrestrial human being. Inside the spiritual cosmos, all of us are weaving, in magnificent spiritual grandeur, the fabric of our own earthly existence, which will be attained by us after descending again into earthly life. Our work, performed in cooperation with the gods, is the fashioning of the earthly human being.

When we speak of seeds here on earth, we think of something small which becomes big. If we speak, however, of the seed of the physical human being as it exists in the spiritual world—for the physical seed maturing in the mother's body is only an image of the spiritual seed—we must think of it as immense, enormous. It is a universe; and all other human beings are interlinked with this universe. It might be said: all human beings are in the same 'place', yet numerically differentiated. And then the spiritual seed diminishes more and more. What we undergo in the time between death and a new birth is the experience of fashioning a spiritual seed, as large as the universe, of our coming earthly existence. Then this spiritual seed begins to shrink until finally it produces its own image in the mother's body.

Materialistic physiology has entirely wrong conceptions of these things. It assumes that the human being, whose marvellous form I have tried to sketch for you, originated simply from a physical human seed. This science considers the ovum to be a highly complicated matter; and physiological chemists investigate the fact that molecules or atoms, becoming more and more complicated, produce the seed, the most complicated phenomenon of all.

All this, however, is not true. In reality, the ovum consists of chaotic matter. Matter, when transformed into a seed, is dissolved; it becomes completely pulverized. The nature of the physical seed, and the human seed particularly, is characterized by being composed of completely pulverized matter, which wants nothing for itself.

Because this matter is completely pulverized and wants nothing for itself, it enables the spiritual seed, which has been prepared for a long time, to enter into it. And this pulverization of the physical seed is brought about by conception. Physical matter is completely destroyed in order that the spiritual seed may be sunk into it and make the physical matter into an image of the spiritual seed woven out of the cosmos.

It is doubtless justified to sing the praises of all that human beings are doing for civilization, for culture, on earth. Far from condemning it, I declare myself, once and for all, in favour of it when it is done in a reasonable way. But a much more encompassing, a much more exalted, a much more magnificent work than all earthly cultural activity is performed by heavenly civilization, as it might be called, between death and a new birth: the spiritual preparation, the spiritual weaving of the human body. For nothing more exalted exists in the world order than the weaving of the human being out of the world's ingredients. With the help of the gods, the human being is woven during the important period between death and a new birth.

If yesterday I said that, in a certain sense, all the experience and knowledge acquired by us on earth provide nourishment for the cosmos, I must say today that, having offered the cosmos as nourishment or fuel all the earthly experiences that could be of use to it, we receive from the fullness of the cosmos all the substances out of which we are able to weave again the new human being into whom we shall enter at a later time.

The human being, now devoting himself wholly to a spiritual world, lives as a spirit. His entire weaving and existence is spiritual work, spiritual essence. This stage lasts for a long time. For it must be repeated again and again: to weave something like the human being is a mighty and grandiose task. Not without justification did the ancient Mysteries call the human physical body a temple. The greater the insight we gain into the science of initiation, into what takes place between death and a new birth, the deeper we feel the significance of this word. Our life between death and a new birth is such that we, as spiritual beings, become directly aware of other spiritual beings. This condition lasts for some time. Then a new stage sets in.

What took place previously was of such a nature that the single spiritual beings could really be viewed as individualities. The spiritual beings with whom one worked were met face to face, as it were. At a later stage, however, these spiritual entities—to express it pictorially, because such things can be suggested only in images—become less and less distinct, finally merging into an aggregation of spirits. This can be expressed in the following way. A certain period between death and a new birth is spent in immediate proximity to spiritual beings. Then comes a time when one experiences only the revelation of these spiritual beings, when they become manifest to us as a whole. I want to use a very trivial metaphor. On seeing what seems to be a tiny grey cloud in the distance, you would be sure that this was just a tiny grey cloud. But by coming closer you would recognize it to be a swarm of midges. Now you can see each single midge. In the case of the spiritual beings, the opposite took place. First you behold the divine spiritual beings, with whom you are working, as single individualities. Then, after living with them more intensively, you behold their general spiritual atmosphere, just as you beheld the swarm of midges in the shape of a cloud. Here, where the single individuals disappear more and more, you live—I might say—in pantheistic fashion in the midst of a general spiritual world.

Although we live now in a general spiritual world, we feel arising out of our inner depth a stronger sense of self-awareness than we experienced before. Formerly your self was constituted in such a way that you seemed to be at one with the spiritual world, which you experienced by means of its individualities. Now you perceive the spiritual world only as a general spiritual atmosphere. Your own self-awareness, however, is perceived to a greater degree. It awakens with heightened intensity. And thus, slowly and gradually, the desire of returning to earth again arises in the human being. This desire must be described in the following way. During the entire period which I have described and which lasts for centuries, the human being is fundamentally interested in nothing but the spiritual world once he has returned to his starting point—except in the first stage when he was still connected with the earth. He weaves, in the large scale which I have described, the fabric of mankind.

At the moment when the individualities of the spiritual world are merged together, as it were, and the human being perceives the spiritual world in a general way, there arises in him a renewed interest in earth life. This interest for earth life appears in a certain specialized manner, in a certain concrete manner. Human beings begin to be interested in definite persons living below on earth, and again in their children, and again in their children's children. Whereas human beings were formerly interested only in heavenly events, they now become, after beholding the spiritual world as a revelation, strangely interested in certain successive generations. These are the generations leading to our own parents, who will bear us on our return to earth. Yet we are interested a long time before that in our parents' ancestors. We follow the line of generations until reaching our parents. Not only do we follow each generation as it passes through time, but—once the spiritual world has been manifested to us as a revelation—we also foresee, as if prophetically, the whole span of generations. Across the succession of great-great-great-grandfathers, great-great-grandfathers, great-grandfathers, grandfathers, and so forth, we can foresee the path on which we shall descend again to earth. Having first grown into the cosmos, we grow later into real, concrete human history. And thus comes the moment when we gradually with regard to our consciousness leave the sun sphere.

Of course, we still remain within the sun sphere; but the distinct, clear, conscious relation to it becomes dim and we are drawn back into the moon sphere. And here, in the moon sphere, we find the 'small package' left by us—I can describe it only by means of this image; we find again what represents the worth of our moral qualities. And this package must be retrieved.

It will be seen in the course of the next days what a significant part is played in this connection by the Christ impulse. We must incorporate within us this package of destiny. But while incorporating within us the package of destiny and entering the moon sphere, while gaining a stronger and stronger feeling of self-awareness and transforming ourselves inwardly more and more into soul beings, we gradually lose the tissue woven by us out of our physical body. The spiritual seed woven by ourselves is lost at the moment when the physical seed, which we shall have to become on earth, is conceived.

The spiritual seed of the physical body has already descended to earth, whereas we still dwell in the spiritual world. And now a vehement feeling of bereavement sets in. We have lost the spiritual seed of the physical body. This has already arrived below and united itself with the last of those successive generations which we have watched. We ourselves, however, are still above. The feeling of bereavement becomes intense. And now this feeling of bereavement draws out of the universe the ingredients of the world ether we need. Having sent the spiritual seed of the physical body down to earth and remained behind as a soul (ego and astral body), we draw etheric substance out of the world ether and form our own etheric body. And approximately three weeks after fertilization has taken place on earth, the physical seed which formed itself out of the spiritual seed is joined to this etheric body, formed by ourselves, as I have previously described.

But before uniting ourselves with our physical seed, we still form our etheric body as I described. And into this etheric body is woven the small package containing our moral worth. We weave this package into our ego, our astral body, and also into our etheric body. Thus it is joined to the physical body. In this way, we bring our karma down to earth. First, it was left behind in the moon sphere; for had we taken it with us into the sun sphere we would have formed a diseased, a disfigured physical body.

The human physical body only acquires individuality through being permeated by the etheric body. Otherwise all physical bodies would be exactly alike; for human beings, while dwelling in the spiritual world, weave identical spiritual germs for their physical body. We become individualities only by means of our karma, by means of the small package interwoven by us with our etheric body which shapes, constitutes and pervades our physical body already during the embryonic stage.

Of course, I shall have to enlarge during the next days on this sketch concerning the human being's transition between death and a new birth. Yet you will have realized what a wealth of experiences is undergone by us: the great experience of how we are first merged into the cosmos and then, out of the cosmos, again are shaped in order to attain a new human earth life.

Fundamentally, we pass through three stages. First, we dwell as spirit-soul among spirit-souls. This is a genuine experiencing of the spiritual world. Secondly, we are given a revelation of the spiritual world. The individualities of the single spiritual entities become blurred as it were. The spiritual world is revealed to us as a whole. Now we approach again the moon sphere. Within ourselves the feeling of self-awareness awakens in preparation of earthly self-awareness. Whereas we did not desire earth life while being conscious of our spiritual self within the spiritual world, we now begin during the period of revelation to desire earth life and develop a vigorous self-awareness directed towards the earth.

In the third stage, we enter the moon sphere and, having yielded our spiritual seed to the physical world, draw together out of all the heavens the etheric substance needed for our own etheric body. Three successive stages: a real life within the spiritual world; a life amidst the revelations of the spiritual world, in which we feel ourselves already as an egoistic self; a life drawing together the world ether.

13. The human being and his pattern in the stars

It is not surprising that astronomers report that there are millions of stars—if we look at it not in terms of vast distances of space, but of a picture of groups of souls. This beautiful description of how we are connected to one another in the cosmos goes beyond any notion of 'sun signs'. There is no reason to suppose that only the zodiacal stars are intended, unless other stars relate to the zodiac in ways at present unknown to us. Unfortunately Steiner did not enlarge on this.

Another question in regard to the relationship of the living to the dead frequently arises: what is the real difference in the relationship between persons when they are both incarnated in physical bodies, when only one of them is, or when neither is? I should here like to say something important about this from a particular point of view.

When with the aid of spiritual science we observe the human being with regard to his ego and to his soul life, or astral body—I have often said of the ego that it is the youngest, the baby, among the members of the human organism, whereas the astral body is somewhat older, though dating only from the moon evolution—we must say of these two highest principles that they are not as yet so far advanced for the human being to rely on them alone for power to maintain himself independently of other human beings. If we were here with one another, each only as ego and astral body, we should be together as though in a sort of primordial jelly.

Our entities would merge into each other; we should not be separate and would not know how to distinguish ourselves one from the other. There would be no possibility of knowing whether a hand or leg were one's own or another's (of course it would all be quite different—these comparisons cannot really be drawn). We could not even properly recognize our feelings as our own. The fact that we perceive ourselves as separate beings depends on our having been drawn out of a fluid continuum—that is how we must picture it for a certain early period—in the form of drops, in such a way that the individual souls did not run together again; we must imagine each soul drop enclosed as though in a piece of sponge. Something like that really occurred. Only because we as human beings are in etheric and physical bodies are we separated from one another, properly separated. In sleep we are kept separate only by a strong longing for our physical bodies. This longing, which draws us ardently to the physical body, divides us in sleep; otherwise we should drift through one another all night long. It would probably be much against the grain of sensitive minds if they knew how strongly they come into connection with other beings in their neigh-bourhood. This, however, is not so very bad in comparison with what might happen if this ardent longing for the physical body did not exist as long as the human being is physically incorporated.

We might now ask: what divides our souls from souls during the time between death and rebirth? Well, as with our ego and astral body between birth and death we belong to a physical and etheric body, so after death, until rebirth, we are part of quite definite starry patterns, no two of them iden-tical; each one of us belongs to a quite distinct pattern. From out of this instinct we speak of 'a person's star'. The whole starry structure, if we take first its physical projection, is globular, but we can divide it in the most varied ways. The regions overlap, but each appertains to another. Expressed spiritually, we might say that each region belongs to a different group of archangels and angels. Just as people here are drawn together through their souls, so between death and rebirth each belongs to a particular starry pattern, to a particular group of angels and archangels; their souls meet together there. The reason why this is apparently so—but I will not go further into this mystery now—is because on earth each soul has his own physical body. I say 'apparently' and you will wonder; but research does surprisingly reveal how to each soul belongs a particular starry pattern, and how the patterns overlap. Let us think of a particular group of angels and archangels. In the life between death and rebirth, thousands of angels and archangels belong to one soul; imagine only one of all these thousands taken away and replaced by another, and we have the region of the next soul.

In this diagram two souls have, with one exception in each case, the same stars; but no two souls have identical structures. Thus human beings are individualized between death

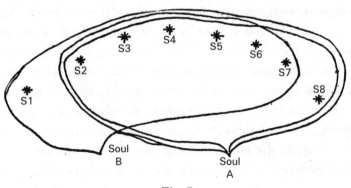

Fig. 7

and rebirth, by having each his special starry pattern. From this we can see how the separation of souls between death and rebirth is effected. In the physical world, as we know, it is effected by the physical body. The human being lives in his physical body as though in a sheath, he observes the world from it, and everything has to come to him through it. All that comes into the soul of the human being between death and rebirth, with regard to the relation between his astral body and his ego, is connected with a certain starry region in a way similar to the connection of the soul and the ego with the physical body during life on earth. Thus the question as to how this separation comes about is answered in the way I have just explained.

From these considerations we have seen today how we can work upon our souls in forming certain feelings and perceptions, so that a bridge of communication may be formed between the so-called dead and the living. What has just been said is also well suited to call up thoughts—one might call them perceptive thoughts or thoughtful perceptions—which can in their turn have a share in the creation of this bridge. This will occur through our seeking more and more to form with regard to some particular dead friend a kind of perception which, when we have experienced something, can call up in the soul the impulse to ask ourselves: 'How would our dead friend experience what I am experiencing at this moment?' By creating the imagination that the dead person is experiencing the event side by side with us and making this a really living feeling, we can form some impression of how intercourse arises between the dead and the living on the one hand and, on the other, between the dead themselves, if we consider how the various starry regions are related to our own souls or to each other. In this way we can gain a feeling for the influences that play from soul to soul because of their relation to certain starry regions.

If we concentrate through the presence of the dead upon an immediate interest, if in this way we feel the dead living close beside us, then from such things as I have discussed today we become more and more conscious that the dead really do approach us. The soul will develop an awareness of this. In this connection we must have confidence that these things really are so, for if we lack confidence and are impatient with life, another truth prevails: the good effects that confidence can bring are driven away by impatience; the enlightenment that comes through confidence is darkened by impatience. Nothing is worse than letting impatience conjure up a mist before the soul.

14. The forces of the earth and the constellation at birth in determining human characteristics

In spite of Steiner's more negative comments on astrology as commonly practised, as we have seen, he showed that there is a connection between human destiny and the birth horoscope, and on occasions he made use of horoscopes himself. In 1924 he visited the newly opened home in Lauenstein, Germany for children with special needs[56] and saw the children in order to give insights from spirit vision as to their treatments. In some cases he asked his colleague Elisabeth Vreede to cast their horoscopes. This is a published example, which indicates his approach. It will be rather too vague for a conventional astrologer; indeed, Elisabeth Vreede remarked that she could not see anything very remarkable in the charts, so Steiner was evidently employing higher faculties in order to read them. However, his conclusions reveal important considerations such as the significance, principally the geology, of the earth itself in the region of birth.

Steiner then goes on to connect the different human 'elements' with the planets (see Theosophy[57] *for a fuller description of these). It is especially interesting because he includes the two outer planets Uranus and Neptune—Pluto was not discovered until 1932—which he rarely mentions. He refers to them as having been drawn into the solar system at a later stage of evolution than the other planets. Now we are shown that they have a bearing on the human being's higher development: the transformations of astral body to Spirit Self; the etheric body to Life Spirit; and the physical body to Spirit Man—developments which will only take place in the distant future. (See* Theosophy. *An explanation here would take us too far from the theme.) A surprising consensus exists among astrologers in general that these outer planets are connected to a person's higher or more spiritual faculties, often with the proviso that the connections may be perceived as negative if these faculties are either denied or not developed, or that they can affect an individual with regard to his or her health, as in the case of these two sisters. It should be noted here that the 'tropical' signs are used, not the actual constellations, which gives validity to Elisabeth Vreede's statement that we can read earthly destiny from the signs and spiritual experiences from the constellations.*[58]

Tomorrow we will speak about the other cases that you have at Lauenstein[59] and I shall be particularly glad to be able to consider with you the interesting phenomenon of albinism, which we have opportunity to study in two of your children. One of them is 15 years old and the other a much younger sister of hers. [Dr Steiner asked Dr Vreede[60] if she had drawn their horoscopes, and she handed them to him. The dates were 6 December 1909, approximately 4 a.m., and 18 May 1921, approximately 3 a.m., both at Jena.] How does Uranus stand? Did you not find any special constellations? [Dr Vreede replied that she had, namely, with Uranus and Neptune. In the case of the elder girl, Neptune was in opposition to Uranus.]

Such children always show two main characteristic peculiarities: very fair hair and poor sight, with the change in the eyes. These are the essential phenomena of albinism. No more than a superficial study is required to discover that in people with albinism we are dealing with an organization that is very weak at assimilating iron but on the other hand assimilates sulphur with the greatest ease. The organization

resists iron, it resists dealing with it, and this applies especially to the periphery of the body; assimilation of iron stops
short of the periphery. Sulphur, on the other hand, is driven
to the periphery, and not only so, but driven even out beyond
it. That is how it comes about that in the region of the hair
you see, all around, a sulphur aura, which pales and bleaches
the hair and takes the strength out of it. And in the eyes
(which develop comparatively independently, being built
into the organism from without, in the embryonic period)—
in the eyes you have a still more striking manifestation of a
sulphur aura. Here it has the effect of fairly forcing the eyes to
take themselves out of the etheric into the astral. In such
children we see the eye plucked right out of its 'grotto', the
etheric body of the eye left disregarded and its astral body
very much to the fore and fully engaged.

Very important questions arise at this point. If we consider
the way the human organism is formed, we find that the
human being is connected on the one hand with the forces
that are in the earth and that divulge themselves to us in the
substances of the earth, and on the other hand with the whole
cosmos. He is dependent on both. Both sets of forces are
present in the individual and karmic process of evolution, as
well as also in the stream of heredity. In considering these
two children, let us take first the stream of heredity. Neither
in the case of the father nor of the mother is there any indication of albinism. They are both perfectly normal human
beings. There was however somewhere in the antecedents—
was it a grandmother, of whom it is reported that she had
signs of albinism? [Dr K.: 'It was a sister of the mother.'] An
aunt, then. Albinism has been known in the family; that is all
that need concern us at the moment. A tendency to albinism
is present in the antecedents. And did you not tell me that

there had been other cases in the Saale region, also at Jena? [Dr K.: 'Yes, two children; and one adult, aged 32, who is already married. Of these three, in only one case had there been albinism previously in the family history.'] It would seem, therefore, that albinism is in some way endemic to a certain part of the country, but meets also with many counterinfluences. And so in fact it makes its appearance quite sporadically! Only under certain circumstances will a person be born there with albinism. The question arises: how does it come about that a person with albinism is born in a particular territory?

In the case of a person with albinism we have, as we have seen, a sulphurization process working outwards, so that little sulphur islets occur in the aura, in the periphery. And now we look round in the native environment of the children to see where we can find sulphur. The whole valley of the Saale abounds in iron sulphide. Iron and sulphur are thus present in combination. You can study first the presence of iron in the vicinity, and then again the presence of sulphur; and you can take special note of the whereabouts of the beautiful pyrites (iron sulphide). These delicate and lovely cubes of pyrites with their beautiful golden lustre are a characteristic product of the valley of the Saale. Other regions nearby yield gypsum. Gypsum is, as you know, calcium sulphate with 20 per cent water. So that here again we have an opportunity to study sulphur—this time in combination with calcium. This kind of study of the soil will throw a light for us on all that lives in the atmosphere and so on, and so we shall have first of all to study that which comes out of the soil and is connected with the absorption of sulphur and iron. For we have here a territory that is also very rich in iron, and the question arises: how does this opposite relationship come about in this territory in regard to earth and the human being, in that the earth has a great power of attraction for iron while the human being cannot attract iron at all, or only with difficulty? What constellations must be present to cause the human being to be particularly disposed to reject the iron and accept the sulphur?

Here we come into the realm of the cosmic; we have to set about investigating the constellations that were present at birth (we cannot of course do it for conception). And this will lead us to ask whether there were not in the case of these children who have albinism quite special constellations, constellations moreover that can only seldom occur. We shall have to find what we can learn, not from the planets that move more quickly but from the constellations of the planets that take a long time to revolve, such as Saturn and Uranus. You see, therefore, to what kind of questions such cases will lead us. We must first find the right questions to ask; once we have the questions, then we are ready to begin our study.

I was speaking to you yesterday about the children with albinism, and I came to the point where I said we need to find the cosmic impulse that can have influence in such cases. Let us begin by asking our expert on cosmic constellations whether she has noticed anything special in these or other horoscopes that people with albinism have in common. [To Dr Vreede] Did you notice that, among the outer planets, Uranus and Neptune were particularly prominent? [Dr Vreede replied: 'Yes, there are many such aspects. Apart from that, there is nothing else I could say about the horoscopes.'] I asked you on purpose because you are frequently engaged in the contemplation of horoscopes and have probably often thought about such things. So far I have from you only these two that we are considering. We are here treading new ground, and it will be best if we go forward entirely in the spirit of discovery. A great many other things are also involved, but I would like us for the moment to consider the following.

Consider the human being. We divide him into certain elements. In accordance with the structure which organizes the whole nature of the human being to a greater extent from the etheric principle, we divide him, as you know, into physical body, etheric body, sentient body, which we then bring into relation with sentient soul; after that we have the intellectual or mind soul (which the Greeks call soul of force or power) and the consciousness soul. And then we come to Spirit Self, Life Spirit and Spirit Man. And all these various elements reveal themselves to us as forming together a single, relatively independent whole; taken all together, they compose the human being. But now, the way in which these elements are put together to compose the human being differs in each single person. One person will have a little more power and strength in his etheric body, and correspondingly less in his physical body; another a little more power in the consciousness soul, and so on. And right in the midst of all these elements we have the human being in his essential individuality, which goes through repeated earth lives, and who must regulate all these elements for himself on the basis of the principle of freedom.

And now let us see how that which comes to the human being from cosmic realms unites itself with these various elements. The influence of the sun, which works strongly on the human being as a whole, works strongest of all on the physical body. In connection with the etheric body we find that the strongest influences come from the moon; in connection with the sentient body it is the influences of Mercury that work with special strength; and in the sentient soul we have the strongest influences of Venus. The strongest influences of Mars serve to help the development of the intellectual or mind soul, and of Jupiter the consciousness soul, while Saturn brings its influences to bear especially on the Spirit Self. And that which has not yet developed in the human being is supported by Uranus and Neptune—the vagrants, so to speak, among the planets, who attached themselves at a later time to our planetary system. In Uranus and Neptune therefore we shall expect to find planetary influences which, under normal conditions, exert no very strong influence upon the constellation at birth.

Spirit Man	♆	Neptune
Life Spirit	♅	Uranus
Spirit Self	♄	Saturn
Consciousness soul	♃	Jupiter
Intellectual soul	♂	Mars
Sentient soul	♀	Venus
Sentient body	☿	Mercury
Etheric body	☽	Moon
Physical body	☉	Sun

You know, of course, from other anthroposophical lectures about the strength of the moon's influence on the human being, via the etheric body. I need not remind you of how the moon is connected with the whole principle of heredity, of how it impresses all manner of forces and powers into the model of the physical body, which comes from the parents. Beginning with the earliest embryonic development, this moon influence determines the whole direction that development shall take in the child.

Now it is possible for a constellation to exist in a person in which the impulse from the moon is strongest, or at least sufficiently strong, for the human being descending to earth to receive by way of heredity a disposition which draws him down into the metabolic organization. Or again, it can also happen that the moon influences are to some extent wrested away, turned aside, while influences that come from quite another quarter and that refuse to tolerate the moon influences, namely Uranus and Neptune, attract what should really be in the sphere of the moon's influence. Other constellations are also possible. But in the case of the children we are considering, the latter is the constellation that we find; and we have here a clear instance of how by looking at what the horoscope shows we can see what is really the matter.

Take first this horoscope (of the elder sister). It will probably have struck you that you find here in this region Uranus together with Venus and Mars. You will not really need to go beyond this trigon. Here, then, are Mars, Venus and Uranus. Consider first Mars. For this child, who was born in 1909, Mars stands in complete opposition to the moon. Mars itself, which has Venus and Uranus in its vicinity, is in strong opposition to the moon. Here is the moon and here is Mars. And Mars drags Uranus and Venus along with it.

And now I would ask you to pay careful attention also to the fact that the moon is at the same time standing before Libra. This means the moon has comparatively little support from the zodiac, it wavers and hesitates, it is even something of a weakling in this hour; and its influence is still further reduced through the fact that Mars (which drags the luciferic influence along with it) stands in opposition to it.

Now let us turn to the horoscope of the younger child. Again, here are Venus and Uranus and Mars near together, the three of them covering between them no more than this section of the heavens. So you see, once again these three are found near to each other. In the case of the elder girl we saw that they were standing in opposition to the moon, which was at the time standing in Libra. On this second horoscope, Mars, Venus and Uranus are in close proximity, exactly as before. But when we examine the position of Mars more precisely, we find it is not, as before, in complete opposition to the moon. But it is approaching opposition. Although the younger child is not in complete opposition, there is an approximation to opposition.

But what strikes us as still more remarkable is that when we come to make our observation of the moon we discover it is again in Libra—while being at the same time, as we have seen, almost in opposition to Mars, the latter dragging Uranus and Venus along with it. We have therefore again a background of Libra. I am not saying that it must have been so; we have, you see, no properly authorized records of the births. On the first horoscope the moon is in Libra, and here on the second too. [Dr Vreede said: 'It is notable that in both there is also the same constellation between moon and Neptune.'] That would have to be explained on its own account. Horoscopes require to be interpreted quite individually. It is no surprise that there is this similarity between the two horoscopes, considering that the girls are sisters. That we find in the elder child a stronger opposition than in the younger (who has been influenced by the elder) is also no cause for astonishment. What is important for us is that we find here a constellation that is perfectly intelligible, a constellation that, when interpreted, shows us the following.

Mars, which is the bearer of iron, makes itself independent of the principle of reproduction—independent, that is, of the moon. It deflects from its true mission that which comes to the human being through the Venus principle and is connected with love. Mars deflects this from its true task, does not allow it to be connected with reproduction and, subsequently, growth. As a result everything which should properly be connected with the growth forces and should live in the lower part of the body pushes up into the head. Consequently we find that in the growth process that takes place within the child iron is lacking, whereas everything that tends to be in conflict with iron, notably sulphur, will be present to excess.

15. The revelation of the stars at death

Not only is a birth horoscope significant but here Rudolf Steiner introduces the conventionally unfamiliar idea that we can equally study the horoscope for the moment of a person's death, that this will reveal much about the significance of their life and what they are offering back to the spiritual world. Willi Sucher, a pioneer in the field of anthroposophical astrology, which he called astrosophy, made many such studies.[61]

To turn now to the discarnate human being, what we call a dead human being, perhaps we need a different kind of consideration. Our method of consideration must remain more mobile. Also there are various points of view from which we could conduct our considerations, for life between death and a new birth is just as complicated as life between birth and death. So let us start with the relationship between the human being here on earth and the human being who has entered the spiritual world through death.

Once again we have the first part, but it is temporal rather than spatial. We could call it the first phase of a development. The dead human being goes, you might say, out into the spiritual world in a certain way; he leaves the physical world but, especially during the first few days, is still very much connected with it. It is very significant that the dead person leaves the physical world in close connection with the constellation arising for his life from the positions of the planets. For as long as the dead person is still connected with his etheric body, the constellation of planetary forces resounds and vibrates in a wonderful way through this etheric body. Just as the territorial forces of the earth vibrate very strongly with the waters of the womb that contains a growing physical human being, so in a most marked way do the forces of the starry constellations vibrate in the dead person who is still in his etheric body at the moment—which is, of course, karmically determined—when he has just left the physical world.

Investigations are often made—unfortunately not always with the necessary respect and dignity, but out of egoistic reasons—into the starry constellation prevailing at birth. Much less selfish and much more beautiful would be a horoscope, a planetary horoscope made for the moment of death. This is most revealing for the whole soul of the human being, for the entry into death at a particular moment is most revealing in connection with karma.

Those who decide to conduct such investigations—the rules are the same as those applied to the birth horoscope—will make all kinds of interesting discoveries, especially if they have known the people for whom they do this fairly well in life. For several days the dead person bears within himself, in the etheric body he has not yet discarded, an echoing vibration of what comes from the planetary constellation. So the first phase is that of the direction in the starry constellation. It is meaningful as long as the human being remains connected with his etheric body.

16. Human and cosmic rhythms

We are related to the cosmos in ways other than by zodiacal signs and planets. Here we see the remarkable way in which our breathing rhythm has a cosmic correspondence. Then Steiner goes on to consider the significance of the lunar nodes, those points which mark the intersection of the sun and moon's paths in relation to the earth and at which eclipses occur, sometimes also called the Dragon's Head and Tail. As explained, this axis is brought about by the oscillation of the earth's axis called nutation. *Some western astrologers and certainly Indian astrologers pay much attention to these as indicators of karma but here we have a greater picture of their spiritual significance. How this rhythm relates to precession is then discussed. The whole extract is a beautifully succinct summary of the way the human being's rhythm fits into the vaster macrocosmic rhythm.*

We shall now have to consider a correspondence that is found to exist, an absolute correspondence, in respect of number. I have already often drawn your attention to this correspondence between the human being and the world in which he evolves. I have pointed to the fact that our rhythm of breathing—18 breaths per minute—manifests something that is in remarkable accord with other processes of the universe. We take 18 breaths per minute, which over a whole day comes to 25,920 respirations. And we arrive at the same number when we calculate how many days are contained in a normal life term of 72 years. That also gives about 25,920 days; so that something may be said to exhale our astral body and ego on falling asleep, and inhale them again upon waking—always in conformity with the same number rhythm.

And again, when we consider how the sun moves— whether apparently or really does not matter—advancing a little each year in what we call the precession of the equinoxes, when we consider the number of years it takes the sun to make this journey round the whole zodiac, once more we get 25,920 years—the Platonic year.

The fact is that within the boundaries set by birth and death this human life of ours is indeed fashioned, down to its most infinitesimal processes—as we have seen in breathing— in accordance with the laws of the universe. But in the correspondence we have observed up to now between the macrocosm and the human being, the microcosm, we have made our observations in a realm where the correspondence is obvious and evident. There are, however, other very important correspondences. For example, consider the following. I want to lead you through number to something else. Take the 18 respirations per minute, making 1080 per hour and in 24 hours 25,920 respirations; that is, we must multiply 18 × 60 × 24 in order to arrive at 25,920.

Taking this as the cycle of the precession of the equinoxes, and dividing it by 60 and again by 24, we would naturally get 18 years. And what do these 18 years really mean? Consider—these 25,920 respirations correspond to a human day of 24 hours; in other words, this 24-hour day is the day of the microcosm. Eighteen respirations may serve as the unit of rhythm.

And now take the complete circle described by the precession of the equinoxes, and call it not a Platonic Year but a great day of the heavens, a macrocosmic day. How long would one respiration on this scale have to occupy to correspond with human respiration? Its duration would have to be 18 years—a respiration made by the being of the macrocosm.

Taking the statements of modern astronomy—we need not interpret them here, we shall speak of their meaning later—let us now examine what modern astronomers call nutation of the earth's axis.

You are aware that the earth's axis lies obliquely upon the ecliptic, and that astronomers speak of an oscillation of the earth's axis around this point and they call this 'nutation'. The axis completes one revolution around this point in just about 18 years (it is really 18 years, 7 months, but we need not consider the fraction, although it is quite possible to calculate this too with exactitude). But with these 18 years something else is intimately connected. For it is not merely on the fact of 'nutation'—this 'trembling', this rotation of the earth's axis in a double cone around the earth's centre, and the period of 18 years for its completion—it is not only on this fact that we have to fix our minds, but we find that simultaneously with it another process takes place. The moon appears each year in a different position because, like the sun, it ascends and descends from the ecliptic, proceeding in a kind of oscillating motion again and again towards the equator ecliptic. And every 18 years it appears once more in the same position it occupied 18 years before. You see there is a connection between this nutation and the path of the moon. Nutation is in truth nothing other than the moon's path. It is the projection of the motion of the moon, so that we can actually observe the 'breathing' of the macrocosm. We only need notice the path of the moon in 18 years or, in other words, the nutation of the earth's axis. The earth dances, and in such a manner as to describe a cone, a double cone, in 18 years, and this dancing is a reflection of the macrocosmic breathing. This takes place just as many times in the macrocosmic year as the 18 human respirations during the microcosmic day of 24 hours.

So we really have one macrocosmic respiration per minute in this nutation movement. In other words, we observe this breathing of the macrocosm through nutation or the movement of the moon, and we have before us what corresponds to respiration in the human being. And now, what does all this mean? The meaning of it is that as we pass from waking to sleep, or only from the wholly conscious to the dream state, we enter another world, and in contrast to the ordinary laws of day, years, etc., and also the Platonic Year, we find in this insertion of a moon rhythm something that has the same relationship in the macrocosm that breathing, the semi-conscious process of respiration, has to our full consciousness. We have therefore not only to consider a world which is spread out before us, but another world which projects into and permeates our own.

Just as we have before us a second part of the human organism, when observing the breathing process, namely the rhythmic realm as opposed to the perceptive or head realm, so we have in what appears as the yearly moon motion, or rather the 18-year motion of the moon, the identity between one year and one human respiration; we have this second world interpenetrating our own.

There can therefore be no question of inhabiting only one world. We have the world that we can observe as the world of the senses; but then we have a world, underpinned by other laws, which stands in exactly the same relationship to the world of the senses as our breathing does to our consciousness. And this other world is revealed to us as soon as we interpret in the right way this moon movement, this nutation of the earth's axis.

These considerations should enable you to realize the impossibility of investigating in a one-sided way the laws manifesting in the world. The modern materialistic thinker is in quest of a single system of natural laws. In this he deludes himself. What he should say is, rather, as follows: 'The world of the senses is certainly a world in which I find myself embedded and to which I belong; it is that world which is explained by natural science in terms of cause and effect. But another world interpenetrates this one, and is regulated by different laws. Each world is subject to its own system of laws.' As long as we are of the opinion that one kind of system of laws could suffice for our world, and that all hangs upon the thread of cause and effect, so long shall we be shrouded in complete illusion.

Only when we can perceive from facts such as the moon's motion and nutation of the earth's axis that another world extends into this one—only then are we on the right path.

And now, you see, these are the things in which the spiritual and material, as we call them, touch each other, or let us say the soul world and the material. He who can faithfully observe what is contained within his own self will find the following—and these are things of which humanity must gradually become aware. There are many among you, I imagine, who have already passed the age of 18 years and about 7 months. That was an important moment. Others will have passed twice that number of years—37 years and 2 months—again an important time. After that we have a third very momentous period, 18 years and seven months later, at the age of 55 years and 9 months. Few can notice as yet, not having been trained to do so, the effects and important changes taking place within the individual soul at these times. The nights passed during these periods are the most important nights in an individual's life. It is then that the macrocosm completes its 18 respirations, completes one minute—and we open a window, as it were, facing quite another world. But as I said, people are not yet aware of these points in their lives. Everyone, however, could try to let his mental eye look back over the years he has passed and, if he is over 55 years old, to recognize three such important epochs; others two, and most of you at any rate one! In these epochs events take place, which rush up into this world of ours out of quite a different one. Our world opens at these moments to another world.

If we wish to describe this more clearly, we can say that our world is at these times penetrated anew by astral streams; they flow in and out. Of course this really happens every year, but we are here concerned with the 18 years, as they correspond to the 18 respirations per minute. In short, our attention is drawn through the cosmic clock to the breathing of the macrocosm, in which we are embedded. This correspondence with another world, which is manifested through the motion of the moon, is exceptionally important. Because, you see, the world which at these times projects into our own is the very world into which we pass during our sleep, when the ego and the astral body leave our physical and etheric bodies. It must not be thought that the world composing our everyday environment is merely permeated in an abstract way by the astral world; rather should we say, it breathes in the astral world, and we can observe the astral in this breathing process through the moon's motion or nutation. You will realize that we have here come to something of great significance. If you remember what I said recently, we may put it in the following way. We have, on the one hand, our world as it is generally observed; and we have in addition the materialistic superstition that, for instance, if we gaze upwards we see the sun, a ball of gas, as it is described in books. This is nonsense. The sun is not a ball of gas; but in that place where the sun is, there is something less than empty space—a sucking, absorbing body, in fact, while all around it is that which exerts pressure. Consequently what comes to us from the sun is nothing to do with any product of combustion in the sun, but is a reflection, a raying back of all that the universe has radiated to it.

Where the sun is, is emptier than empty space. This can be said of all parts of the universe where we find ether. For this reason it is so difficult for the physicist to speak of ether, for he thinks that ether is also matter, though more rarefied than ordinary matter. Materialism is still very busy with this perpetual 'rarefying', both the materialism of natural science as well as the materialism of theosophy. It distinguishes first dense matter; then etheric matter—more rarefied; then astral matter—still more rarefied; and then there is the 'mental' and I do not know what else—always more and more rarefied! The only difference (in this theory of rarefying) between the two forms of materialism is that the one recognizes more degrees of rarefaction than the other. But in the transition from quantifiable matter to ether rarefaction plays no part. Anyone who believes that in ether we have to do merely with a 'rarefying' process is like someone who says: 'I have here a purse full of money. I repeatedly take from it and the money becomes less and less. I take away still more till at last none remains, nothing is left.' But in fact one can continue! The 'nothing' can become less still, for if we get into debt our money becomes less than nothing. In the same way not only does matter become empty space, but it becomes negative, less than nothing, emptier than emptiness; it assumes a 'sucking' nature. Ether is sucking, absorbing. Matter presses, ether absorbs. The sun is an absorbing, sucking sphere, and wherever ether is present we have this force of suction.

Here we step over into the other aspect of three-dimensional space—we pass from pressure to suction. That which immediately surrounds us in this world, that of which we are constituted as physical and etheric human beings, is both pressing and sucking or absorbing. We are a combination of both, whereas the sun possesses the power of suction only, being nothing but ether, nothing but suction. It is the undulating wave of pressure and suction, ponderable matter and ether, that forms in its alternation a living organization. And the living organism continually breathes in the astral; the breathing expresses itself through the moon's motion or nutation. And here we begin to divine a second aspect or principle of the world's construction: the one aspect, pressure and suction, physical and etheric; the second, astral. The astral is neither physical nor etheric but is continually inhaled and exhaled; and nutation manifests this.

Now a certain astronomical fact was observed even in most ancient times. Many thousands of years before the Christian era, the Egyptians knew that after a period of 72 years the fixed stars in their apparent course gain one day on the sun. It seems to us, does it not, that the fixed stars revolve and the sun too revolves, but that the latter revolves more slowly, so that after 72 years the stars are appreciably ahead. This is the reason for the movement of the vernal point (the spring equinoctial point), namely that the stars move faster. If the spring equinox moves on and on, the fixed stars must have altered their position in relation to the sun. Briefly, we find that at the end of 72 years the fixed stars are ahead of the sun by one day. For instance, they occupy a particular position on 30 December, while the sun only reaches that point again on 31 December. The sun has lost a day. After a lapse of 25,920 years this loss is so great that the sun has described a complete revolution and once again is back at the position we originally noted. We see therefore that in 72 years the sun is one day behind the fixed stars. Now these 72 years are approximately the normal lifespan of a human being, composed of 25,920 days.

Thus when we multiply 72 years by 360, and consider the human span of life as one day, we have the human life as one day of the macrocosm. The human being is exhaled, as it were, from the macrocosm, and his life is one day in the macrocosmic year.

So that this revolution, this circle described by the precession of the equinoxes, indicating the macrocosmic year, as already known to the Egyptians thousands of years ago (for they looked upon this period of 72 years as very important), this apparent revolution of the vernal point is connected with the human being's life and death in the universe—with the life and death, that is, of the macrocosm. And the laws of the life and death of the human being are something that we must pursue. We have already found how nutation points to another world—as our sense perception world points to one world, so nutation points to another, the breathing world. And now through what present-day astronomy calls 'precession' we have something we may again call a transition, a transition this time to a state of deep sleep, a transition to still another, a third world. We have thus three worlds, interpenetrating one another, interrelated; but we must not attempt simply to link these worlds in a causal way. Three worlds, a threefold world, as the human being is a threefold being: one, the world of sense surrounding us, the world we perceive; a second world whose presence is indicated by the motions of the moon; and a third which makes itself known to us by the motion of the equinoctial point or, we might say, by the path of the sun. This third world indeed remains about as unknown to us as the world of our own will is unknown to our ordinary consciousness.

It is important therefore to search everywhere for correspondences between the human microcosm and the macrocosm. And when people of the East, if only in a decadent way, nowadays seek to acquire breathing consciousness, as was done in ancient oriental wisdom, this is the manifestation of a desire to slip over into this other world—which can otherwise only be recognized through what the moon, so to speak, wills in our world. But in those ancient times, when there was still an ancient wisdom coming to the human being in a different manner from the way in which we have to seek wisdom nowadays—in those times the human being also knew how to see this working of inner laws in other connections and correspondences.

17. Solar and lunar eclipses

From the lunar nodes we pass naturally to the nature of eclipses, which in past times were awaited with great dread. We have only to think of Nostradamus' famous quatrain referring to the total solar eclipse of 1999 as 'a Great King of Terror from the sky'.[62] Steiner gives a rather different picture of a solar eclipse as existing to provide a certain safety valve for human evil deeds, and a lunar eclipse allows for people to receive evil thoughts if they so desire, which may be present in the earth's aura. The idea is that evil will then work in a less concentrated way. Furthermore he encourages us to look at the rays of sun and moon as being spiritual pathways for souls leaving and returning to the earth, expressing a reality that existed as a notion in many ancient cultures.

In addition to all this, a human being who has had these experiences learns to measure the true significance of certain transitory phenomena which stand, as it were, midway between processes regarded as physical and cosmic in their nature, and those which are cosmic and spiritual. The human being of today, owing largely to his materialistic education, describes everything from the physical point of view. He says: 'An eclipse of the sun is due to the fact that the moon comes between the sun and the earth, cutting off the rays of the sun.' This is a physical explanation, built up from physical observation and as obvious as if we were to say: 'Here is a light, and there an eye. If I place my hand in front of the eye, the light will be darkened.' As you see, it is a purely physical, spatial explanation, and that is as far as modern consciousness goes.

We must strive once more for a true knowledge of such phenomena. They are not of everyday occurrence, and on the comparatively rare occasions of their appearance they should be studied not only from their physical but also from their spiritual aspect.

At the time of a solar eclipse, for instance, something totally different takes place in the part of the earth affected from what is happening when there is no eclipse. When we know that on the one hand the rays of the sun penetrate down to the earth and on the other hand the forces or rays of will stream out to meet the sun, it is possible to form some idea of how a solar eclipse can affect these radiations of will which are altogether spiritual in their nature. The sunlight is blocked by the moon; that is a purely physical process. But physical matter—in this case the body of the moon—is no obstacle to the forces streaming out from the will. These forces radiate into the darkness, and there ensues a period of time, short though it may be, in which all that is of the nature of will upon the earth flows out into universal space in an abnormal way. It is different altogether from what takes place when there is no eclipse. Ordinarily, the physical sunlight unites with the radiation of will streaming towards it. When there is an eclipse, the forces of will flow unhindered into cosmic space.

The old initiates knew these things. They saw that at such a moment all the unbridled impulses and instincts of humanity surge out into the cosmos. And they gave their pupils the following explanation. They said: under normal conditions die evil impulses of will which are sent out into the cosmos by human beings are, as it were, burned up and consumed by the rays of the sun, so that they can injure only the human being himself, but can do no universal harm. When, however, there is an eclipse of the sun, opportunity is given for the evil which is willed on earth to spread over the cosmos. An eclipse is a physical event behind which there lies a significant spiritual reality.

And again, when there is an eclipse of the moon, the human being of today merely says: 'Now the earth comes between the sun and the moon; hence we see the shadow cast upon the moon by the earth.' That is the physical explanation. But in this case also the old initiate knew that a spiritual reality lay behind the physical fact. He knew that when there is an eclipse of the moon, thoughts stream through darkness down upon the earth, and that such thoughts have a closer relationship with the subconscious life than with the conscious life of the human being. The old initiates often made use of a certain simile when speaking to their pupils. It is, of course, necessary to translate their words into modern language, but this is the gist of what they said: 'Visionaries and dreamers love to go for rambles by moonlight, when the moon is full. There are, however, certain people who have no wish to receive the good thoughts coming to them from the cosmos, but who, on the contrary, desire to get hold of evil, diabolical thoughts. Such people will choose the moment of a lunar eclipse for their nocturnal wanderings.'

Here again we approach a spiritual reality in a physical event. Today we must not absorb such teaching in its old form. Were we to do so, we should be led into superstition. But it is very necessary to reach a point at which we are able once more to perceive the spiritual which permeates all cosmic processes. Eclipses of the sun and moon, recurring as they do in the course of every year, may really be looked upon as 'safety valves'. A safety valve is there to avert danger, to provide an outlet for something or other—steam, for

instance—at the right moment. One of the safety valves
which makes its appearance in the cosmos and to which we
give the name of a solar eclipse serves the purpose of carrying
out into space in a luciferic way the evil that spreads over the
earth in order that evil may wreak havoc there. The other
safety valve, the lunar eclipse, exists for the purpose of
allowing the evil thoughts which are present in the cosmos to
approach those human beings who desire to be possessed by
them. In matters of this kind people do not, as a rule, act in
full consciousness, but the facts are nevertheless real—just as
real as the attraction of a magnet for small particles of iron.
Such are the forces at work in the cosmos—forces no less
potent than the forces we analyse and investigate today in our
chemical laboratories.

The human being will not be able to free himself from the
forces in his being which tend to drag him downwards until
he develops in himself a certain feeling for spiritual concepts
such as these. Then only will the path leading to a true
comprehension of birth and death be opened up to humanity. And such a comprehension and understanding is sorely
needed by humanity today, when human beings are plunged
in spiritual darkness. We must learn again what it really
signifies when the sun sends its light towards us. When the
sunlight streams towards us, the surrounding space is made
free for the passage of those souls who must leave their
physical bodies and make their way out into universal space.
When the sun sends its light down to earth, the earth sends
human souls out into cosmic space, where these souls
undergo many metamorphoses. Then, in a spiritual form,
they approach the earth once more, passing in their descent
through the sphere of the moon, and taking possession once
again of a physical body which has been prepared for them in

the stream of physical heredity. It will not be possible for us to enter into a right relationship with the universe until such time as we begin to feel and experience these things in a real and living way.

Today we learn astronomy, spectroscopy and so on. We learn how the rays of the sun penetrate down to earth, and we fondly imagine that there is nothing more to be said. We learn how the rays of the sun fall upon the moon, and from the moon are reflected back again to earth, and we look upon the moonlight in this way only, taking into consideration merely its physical aspect. By such means the intellect is brought into play. Intellectual knowledge cuts the human being off from the cosmos, and tends to destroy inner activity of soul. This inner life of soul can be reawakened, but the human being must first win back for himself his spiritual relationship with the cosmos. This he will be able to do only when he is once more able to say to himself: 'A human being has died. His soul is radiating out towards the sun. It streams out into the cosmos, travelling the path made for it by the rays of sunlight, until it comes into a region where space has an end, where one can no longer speak in terms of three dimensions, but where the three dimensions are merged into unity. In this region, beyond space and beyond time, many and various things happen. But later on, from the opposite direction, from the direction of the moon, of the moonlight, the soul returns once more and enters into a physical human body, is born again into earthly life.'

When the human being learns once more that the souls of the dead go out to meet the light rays of the sun, that the shining beams of the moon draw the young souls back again to earth, when he learns to feel concretely how natural processes and phenomena are everywhere permeated with spirit—then there will arise once more on earth a knowledge which is at the same time religion, a truly devotional knowledge.

18. Comets and other cosmic phenomena

Here Steiner discusses comets in a very clear way devoid of any superstition. Then he goes on to speak about the zodiac and gives a concise account of why it is that a constellation has an effect when a planet is moving in front of it—not as usually supposed that it is enhanced in some way, but because the 'blocking' by the planet results in people having to develop those qualities pertaining to the constellation in themselves. He concludes with the true nature of the sun. This lecture was given to the workmen who were erecting the first Goetheanum in Dornach (later destroyed by arson) in answer to questions put by the men. The replies are given in a lively and direct form. Steiner uses the term 'constellation' here and presumably means the actual constellation, not the sign. As with plants, this may be more relevant for health issues, though it does raise questions about the nature of which influences are involved.

Mr Erbsmehl: What do the comets mean that appear from time to time? And how is the zodiac different from other stars?

Rudolf Steiner: This question can help us to gain some understanding of astronomy. You are attending lectures on astronomy, and it may be quite a good thing to discuss this particular issue from a particular point of view.

Looking at the starry heavens [drawing], we see the moon as the largest star, which is also closest to us. The moon's influence on human beings on earth is therefore also most easily apparent. And you'll no doubt have heard people say how the moon stimulates people's imagination. This is something everyone knows. But I have told you of other influences the moon has, on reproduction, too, and so on. Then we see other heavenly bodies that behave in a similar way to the moon. The moon moves—you can see it move—and other stars, which are similar to it, also move. These stars, which also move, we call wandering stars or planets.

Now the sun also appears to move. And it does indeed move. But relative to our earth it does not move. It is always at about the same distance and it does not orbit the earth. The sun is therefore called a fixed star. And all other stars, except for those that clearly change their position, are also fixed stars.

Looking at the starry heavens we see more or less what we see when we look at them every night—especially on moonlit nights. But there are changes in the heavens. During certain weeks in summer in particular you can see one star after the other—seemingly—moving swiftly across the sky and disappearing: falling stars. They also appear in the sky on other occasions, but are particularly visible in some weeks during the summer when swarms of such small stars light up, pass rapidly across the sky and vanish.

Apart from them there are the stars to which Mr Erbsmehl referred in his question—the comets. These comets appear less often; they also differ from other stars in their form. Their shape is something like this [drawing]. They have a kind of nucleus and then a tail which follows behind. Sometimes they also appear to have two such tails behind them. If we look at the other stars that move we find their movements to be fairly regular, and we always know that they appear at certain times and at other times are beneath the earth and do not appear. But with these stars, the comets, one sees them coming and going without really ever knowing where they are going. Their movements are therefore irregular, as it were, among the other stars.

Now these comets have always been regarded as something different from other stars by people, and they have played a big role above all among superstitious people. These superstitious people thought that the appearance of a comet signalled disaster.

This should not surprise us, for anything that is irregular causes amazement and surprise. We need not take it too seriously, for people will also consider it to mean something special when objects that normally behave in one way behave differently. If you drop a knife, for example, it will not normally stick in the ground but fall fiat. This does not signify anything, for we are used to it. But if the knife sticks in the ground, superstitious people will think this means something. When the moon appears it is something people are used to and it does not mean anything special. But when such a star appears and, what is more, has a special shape, well, then it does mean something special! So there's no need to get excited when superstitious people think things mean something.

We have to consider the matter in a scientific way. And above all the following is true. In times not that long ago, people went by what they saw in the heavens, and said the earth was the centre of the world (I am merely telling you how people saw it) and that the moon, Mercury, Venus, the sun, and so on, moved around the earth, and that the whole of the starry heavens—as one also can see now, every star rises and sets[63]—was moving. So you see the starry heavens in motion. If you stay outside long enough you'd see the so-called fixed stars move across the sky. People took it the way they saw it in earlier times.

Now, as you know, Copernicus came along in the fifteenth, sixteenth century and said: 'No such thing! The earth is not the centre. The sun is the centre, and Mercury, Venus, earth and so on move around the sun' [drawing]. So the earth itself became a planet. A completely different system, a new way of looking at space, came up. And like the sun, so the other fixed stars were now said to be stationary. Their movements would thus only be apparent movements.

You see, gentlemen, the matter is like this. I spoke of this before, when Mr Burle asked about the theory of relativity, wanting to know if those theories were correct and also some other things that were said. Another theory was established by a man called Tycho Brahe,[64] for instance. He said: 'Yes, the sun is standing still, but the earth is also standing still,' and so on. So there were also other systems. But we'll look at these two, the old one, mainly based on Ptolemy,[65] the Ptolemaic system, and then the Copernican system, which goes back to Copernicus. So there we have two systems of the universe. Each is right in some way. Above all we cannot tell, if we go into these things in detail, if the one is right or the other.

The thing is this, gentlemen. I told you before that some people cannot say, when I drive a car from the Villa Hansi up to the Goetheanum, if the car is moving or the Goetheanum is coming to meet it. Well, it is certainly something you cannot tell by just looking, but only by the fact that the car gets worn, the car uses up petrol, and the Goetheanum does not. You can tell the difference by things that are internal. In the same way you can tell, if you walk to Basel, if Basel is coming towards you or you are going there because you get tired. So it is internal things that tell the difference.

This is only to show you that really every system of the

universe is such that in one respect it may be correct and in another it may be wrong. You cannot tell with absolute certainty. That is how it is. You really cannot say which system of the universe is completely right and which is completely wrong. Ah, you'll say, these things are worked out by calculations! Well, you see, those calculations are made, but the calculations that are made are never entirely correct. If you calculate the rate at which a star moves, for example, you'll know that after a certain time it must be in a particular position in the heavens. So you work out where a star should be at a given time, and you turn your telescope in that direction—now it should appear in the telescope. Often it does not, and then the formula has to be corrected; and so one finds that one's calculations are never quite right. The thing with the universe is that none of our calculations are ever exactly right.

Why is that? Imagine you know someone quite well. You'll say to yourself that if he promises something you can definitely rely on it. Let us assume you know someone pretty well. He has promised to be in a particular place at five in the afternoon on 20 May. You will also be there. You'll be quite sure he'll be there, because you know him. But it may happen after all that he does not turn up. And that is how it is with the system of the universe. Looking at minor things one may say: you can rely on it that things will happen the way you know they will. So if I make a fire in a stove, it will, according to the laws of nature, bring warmth to the room. It is not very probable that a fire will not make a room warm. But this is no longer so, gentlemen, when we get to large-scale events in the universe. The matter then becomes as certain as it is with an individual person, and it also becomes as uncertain as it is with an individual person. So that everything one calculates always has a flaw in it somewhere. And where does this flaw come from? The flaw is not only because these solar systems do not exist on their own. Let us assume the person saw something he really liked as he was on his way to meet you. He was held up. If these planetary systems were such that nothing could happen with them but what sun, moon and stars are doing, we would also be able to calculate them. We would know exactly where a star will be at a particular time, to the thousandth of a second, for calculations can be extremely accurate. But, as I said, there is a flaw. This is simply due to the fact that these systems are not permitted to be entirely free and easy amongst themselves in the universe, for the comets come in, passing right through. And with these comets coming in from the universe, the universe is giving the planetary system something that is rather like what we are given when we eat. The comet is a kind of food for the planetary systems! And it is like this. When such a comet comes in, small changes occur in the movements, and so one never gets an entirely regular movement. So that is the situation, gentlemen. The comets bring irregularity into the state of motion or of rest in our whole planetary system.

Now as to the comets themselves. You see, people will say: 'Yes, such a comet, it comes from so far away that you do not see it at first; you begin to see it when it comes closer to the solar system [drawing]. So there you see it. Now it moves on; you still see it, then you see it a little, and then it vanishes.' So what are people saying? They are saying: 'Well that is above the earth, and one can see it. But then the comet moves over there, becomes invisible, and comes back again there after a number of years.' That is what they say.

If I draw the solar system for you, we have here the sun; here the planets. People imagine that the comet comes from far away, from beyond the solar system, and enters the sphere of the sun; and there you no longer see it, when it is down below. There it comes back again. So they imagine the planets move in short ellipses, and the comet in a tremendously long ellipse. And when it comes and we have it above us, so that one can look up, it is visible; otherwise it is invisible and then comes back again. Halley's comet, called after the man who discovered it,[66] appears every 76 years.

Now, gentlemen, this is something where the science of the spirit cannot agree, because of observations made in it. For it is not true that the comet moves like this. The real truth is that the comet only comes into existence here, and it sunders matter together[67] from the universe; matter from the universe gathers. There it comes into existence [pointing to the drawing], moves on like this, and here it vanishes again, dissolving. This line [ellipse] here, actually does not exist. So we are dealing with a structure that develops some distance away and passes out of existence again at some distance. So what is really going on here?

Now, one gets to the point where one says: it is not true that the sun is standing still. It is standing still in relation to the earth, but it moves at tremendous speed in relation to space. The whole planetary system is rushing through cosmic space, moving forward. The sun is moving towards the constellation of Hercules. Now you may ask how people know that the sun is moving towards Hercules. You know that if you go down an avenue and stand at one end, the trees near you seem further apart, and then they come closer and closer. You know, if you look down an avenue, the trees seem to be closer and closer together; but when you walk in this direction it seems as if they move apart. The distance you see between trees keeps growing. Now imagine this here is

Hercules [drawing], the stars in that constellation are at some distance from one another. If our solar system were standing still, those distances would always be the same. But if the sun were moving towards it, the stars in Hercules would grow bigger and bigger and would appear to move apart. And this is what they actually do! It has been observed through the centuries that the distances in Hercules are getting bigger and bigger. This shows that the sun is truly moving in the direction of Hercules. And just as it is possible to calculate things here, using ranging instruments, how close we are when walking past and how fast we are walking—when someone walks faster, the distance increases faster than it does for someone else—so it is possible to calculate how the sun moves. The calculations are always very accurately done. Our whole planetary system is thus rushing towards the constellation of Hercules.

This rushing pace affects the planetary system just as work does you. Working, you lose some of your substance and need to replace it. And as the planetary system rushes through cosmic space it is also all the time losing some of its substance. This needs to be replaced. So you have the comets moving around. They gather the substance, and it is captured again as the comet passes through the planetary system. Comets thus replace substance for which the planetary system no longer has any use and which it has eliminated. But the comets also cause irregularities as they enter into the planetary system, so that it is in fact not possible to calculate the movements.

This also shows that if you go far enough, things come alive for you in cosmic space. Such a planetary system is really a form of life; it needs to eat. And the comets are eaten!

What do these comets essentially consist of? The most

important substance they contain is carbon and nitrogen, which is indeed something needed in the planetary system and has to come from the heavens. We need nitrogen in the air, and it has to be renewed all the time; we need carbon because all plants need it. And so the earth does truly get its substances from the universe. They are always replaced.

But there's more to this. You know that when you have a meal you eat things that are still quite large when they are on your plate. You reduce them in size by biting. First of all you cut them up. And you have to do this, for if it were possible for you to swallow a goose whole, this would not be good for you! You need to cut it up. You also can't swallow a whole calf's head; only snakes can do that, people cannot. It needs to be cut up. The planetary system also does this with its food. Comets may sometimes—not every one of them, but some can sometimes be swallowed whole, snake fashion. But other comets are broken up when they enter the system. The comet then breaks up, just as a shower of meteors has broken up into lots of small stars. These meteors are tiny parts of comets that rush down. And so you see not only how cosmic food enters into the solar system but also how this cosmic food is consumed by the earth. We are thus able to get a clear idea of the role that comets, which appear at irregular intervals, play for the earth.

Now you see, the thing is like this—we must leave aside all superstition. The comet coming from beyond the earth has an influence on everything that happens on the earth, and this is something we can see. It is certainly a strange thing. As you know, there are good and bad years for wine. But the good years really come because the earth has got hungry. It then leaves its fertility more to the sun, and the sun gives the wine its quality. Now when the earth has had a good wine year, you can be pretty certain that a comet will appear soon after, for the earth has been hungry and needs food again for the other things. You then get poor wine years. If there's another good wine year, a comet will follow. The earth's state concerning its substance is definitely connected with the way in which comets appear or do not appear.

The other question was how the zodiac differs from other fixed stars.

You know, if we simply look out into the distant universe we see countless stars. They seem to be irregularly placed. But one can always distinguish groups of them, and these are called constellations.

Now the stars we see are further away from the moon or closer to it. Looking at the stars we see the moon pass through the starry heavens like this [drawing], don't we? But whilst some constellations are positioned in such a way that the moon always passes through them, it does not pass through others. So if you consider Hercules, for instance, the moon does not pass through. But if you look at the Lion, then the moon always passes through the Lion at given intervals. Twelve constellations have the special characteristic that they form the path, as it were, taken by the moon and also by the sun. We may say, therefore, that the twelve constellations Ram, Bull, Twins, Crab, Lion, Virgin, Scales, Scorpion, Archer, Goat, Water Carrier and Fishes mark the path of the moon. It always passes through them and not through the other constellations. We are thus always able to say that at any particular time the moon, if it is in the sky, is in one constellation or another, but only a constellation that is part of the zodiac.

Now I want you to consider, gentlemen, that everything there is by way of stars in the sky has a definite influence on the earth as a whole and specifically also on the human being. He truly depends not only on what exists here on earth but also on the stars that are there in the heavens.

Think of some star or constellation up there. It rises in the evening, as we say, and sets in the morning. It is there all the time, and always influences the human being. But think of another constellation, the Twins, let us say, or the Lion. The moon passes that way. The moment it passes that way it covers up the Twins or the Lion. I see only the moon and not the Twins. At that moment they cannot influence the earth, because their influence is blocked. And so we have stars everywhere in the sky that are never blocked out, neither by the sun nor by the moon, and always have an influence on the earth. And we have stars which the moon passes, and the sun seemingly also passes them. These are covered up from time to time and their influence then stops. We are therefore able to say that the Lion is a constellation in the zodiac and has a particular influence on the human being. It does not have this influence if the moon is in front of it. At that time the human being is free of the Lion influence, the Lion's influence does not affect him.

Now just imagine you are terribly lazy and won't walk but someone gives you a push from behind, and you have to walk. He drives you on, and that is his influence. But imagine I do not permit him to influence you; he cannot give you a push. Then you are not subject to the influence; and if you want to walk you have to do it yourself.

Human beings need these influences. And how does this go, gentlemen? Let us hold fast to this: the Lion constellation has a particular influence on the human being. It has this influence for as long as it is not covered up by the moon or the sun. But let us take this further. Again consider an analogy from life. Let us say you want to know something. Imagine you have a governess or a private tutor—he usually knows everything. When you are a little boy you don't want to think for yourself, you ask your tutor and he'll tell you. He'll also do your homework for you. But if the tutor has gone out, so that you do not have your tutor available at the moment and have to do your homework, then you have to find the power in yourself. You have to recall things for yourself.

The Lion continually influences human beings except when it is covered by the moon. Then the influence is not there. When the moon blocks the Lion's influence, the human being must develop using his own resources. Someone able to develop his own strong Lion influence when the moon covers the constellation may thus be called a Lion person. Someone able to develop particularly the influence in the constellation of the Crab when this is covered up is a Crab person. People develop the one or the other more strongly depending on their inner constitution.

You see, therefore, that the constellations of the zodiac are special, for with them, the influence is sometimes there and sometimes not. The moon, passing through the constellations at four week intervals, brings it about that there is always a time in a four week period when some constellation of the zodiac does not have an influence. With other constellations the influence is always the same. In earlier times people took these influences that came from the heavens very seriously. The zodiac was therefore more important to them than other constellations. The others have a continuous influence which does not change. But with the zodiac we may say that the influence changes depending on whether one of its constellations is covered over or not. Because of this, the influence of the zodiac on the earth has always been the subject of special study. And so you see why the zodiac is more important when we study the starry heavens than other stars are.

You will see from all this that mere calculations cannot really give us all the knowledge we want of the heavens, as I told you before. We certainly have to consider things like those I have been speaking of.

Talking about such things one is still thought to be a dreamer today, something of a fool, for people say: 'If you want to know something about the stars you should go to the astronomers at the observatory. They know everything!' As you know, there is a saying—because conditions like gout also depend on all kinds of external influences, some people will tell someone with gout to go to the observatory and have the matter sorted there. But when you want to speak of these things out of the spirit today, people think you are something of a fool. But the following kind of thing happens. Having gained knowledge through the science of the spirit, I was able to say the following in a series of lectures I gave in Paris in 1906.[68] If everything is like this with the comets, if they really exist to perform this function, then they must contain a compound of carbon and nitrogen. This was something people did not know before. Carbon and nitrogen combine to form cyanide, prussic acid. Carbon and nitrogen would thus have to be found also in comets. I said this in Paris in 1906. People who did not acknowledge the science of the spirit did not need to believe it at the time. But a short time after this I was on a lecture tour in Sweden and all the papers brought the surprising news that spectroscopic analysis had shown comets to contain cyanide.

You see, people are always saying that if anthroposophists

know something they should say so, so that it may later be confirmed. There have been many such instances. Honestly, I predicted the discovery of cyanide in comets in 1906! It was made soon after. You can see, therefore, that these things are correct, for the truth will be confirmed in due course, if one sets about it in the right way. But of course, when this kind of thing happens again people do not mention it, they hush it up because it does not suit them. But it is true nevertheless. Spiritual perception thus enables us to say things about the comets, including their chemical composition, and this will be confirmed in due course. This is one such example.

So I am not afraid to say things that may seem utterly foolish to people: that the comets come into existence here and pass out of existence again there, gather matter here and vanish again here as they leave the planetary system. Spiritual observation shows this, and in due course physical observation will confirm it. Today one is only able to state it on the basis of spiritual observation.

Many things said in materialistic science today are utterly fantastic. People imagine the sun to be a kind of gaseous sphere, for instance. It is not a gaseous sphere, but really something quite different. You see, gentlemen, if you have a bottle of carbonated water you get those small beads in there. So one might think: right, that is carbonated water, and in it are small beads—things that float in it. But that is not how it really is, for there you have your carbonated water, and there it is hollow [drawing]. You have less in there than in the rest of the water. It is of course carbon dioxide gas, with water all around it, but the gas is thinner than the water. With reference to the water, you have a hollow space in there, and compared to water you merely have the subtle nature of the gas. The sun, too, is a hollow space in the universe; but it is thinner than any gas; it is extremely thin in the place where the sun is. And what is more, gentlemen, when you move around in the world you are in space. But space is also hollow where the sun is. What does it mean: 'space is hollow'? You can see from the following what it means when we say space is hollow.

If you create a vacuum with a vacuum pump, removing all the air [drawing], and then make an opening here, the air rushes in with a tremendous hissing sound. The situation with the sun is that what you have there is definitely above all a hollow space, empty not only of air but also of heat. It is above all a hollow space. The nature of this hollow space is such that it is spiritually closed off all around, and something can rush in only at intervals through the sun spots. Astronomers would get a big surprise if they were to go there in a space car or spaceship—it could not be an airship, of course, for the air does not go as far as that. The astronomers would expect that when they got up there and arrived at the sun they would enter such a nebula, for the sun, they think, is red-hot gas. And they would expect this red-hot gas to burn them up, that they would perish in flames, for they believe they would find a temperature of many thousands of degrees. But you do not get the opportunity to burst into flames, for the sun is hollow also as far as heat is concerned. There is no heat either! One would be able to tolerate all this. One would also be able to tolerate the temperature if one went to the sun in a giant spaceship. But something else could not be tolerated. The situation would be similar to the air rushing in with a hiss—rushing in, not out—and you would immediately be drawn into the sun and would instantly turn to dust, for the sun is a hollow space that sucks in everything. You would be completely absorbed. It would be the most certain way of disappearing.

The sun is thus seen entirely in the wrong light by materialistic scientists. It is a hollow space with regard to anything else; and this really makes it the lightest body among all the stars nearest to us out there in space, lightest of all. The moon is relatively heavy, for it once came away from the earth, taking with it the heavy substances for which the earth had no use. It would be lighter than the earth, of course, if we were to weigh it, being much smaller, but relatively speaking, in terms of what we call the specific gravity, it is heavier. It follows that spirituality comes from the sun, for it is the lightest body in cosmic space. This is why I was able to say, when Mr Dollinger asked about the Christ, that the greatest spirituality comes from the sun when we are born, for the sun is the most spiritual entity. The moon is the most material entity. And if the moon is the most material body, its influence on human beings goes beyond the ordinary in material terms. You see, all the other stars apart from the moon also have an influence, of course. They have an influence on material processes. But if you imagine you're eating a piece of bread, the bread is gradually transformed into blood; something is transformed into something else. Part of the human being is created, blood is created, when you transform bread in the metabolic process. If you put salt in your bread, the salt goes into the bones; it is transformed. It is always a part that is produced, for these materials relate only to parts of the human being. All things on earth can only create part of the human being; and whatever is produced must remain in the human being. The moon itself has a powerful material influence on reproduction, but in that case it is not part of the human being that is produced but a whole human being. The sun influences the most spiritual part, the moon, being material itself, the material aspect. The human being thus creates himself, or an image of himself, under the influence of the moon. That is the difference. Sun actions may be said to recreate our thoughts, our powers of will all the time. The moon's influence is that it recreates the material forces, reproducing the material human being. And between the sun and the moon we have the other stars which bring about parts of the other things that happen in the human being.

We can understand all this. But you must include the human being whenever you consider astronomy. You see, an astronomer will say: 'What I see with my naked eye does not impress me; I have to use a telescope. I rely on my telescope; it is my instrument.' The spiritual scientist will say: 'Why bother with telescopes! Of course you'll see a great deal, and we acknowledge this. But the best instrument you can use to gain insight into the universe is the human being himself.' You perceive everything through the human being. The human being is the best instrument, for everything becomes apparent in him. What happens up there in the Lion is apparent in the circulation of the blood. And when the moon is in front of the Ram, our hair grows more slowly, and so on. It is always possible to see in the human being what happens in the universe. When someone gets jaundice, for instance, we must of course primarily use medicine to consider the cause in the body. But why, in the final instance, does a person get jaundice? Because he has a special disposition to develop the powers of the Goat from his own resources when the moon covers up the constellation of the Goat.

We can thus always see that the human being is the instrument by which all may be perceived. When a person is no longer open, for instance, to the Water Carrier influence, that is if the Water Carrier is covered up by the moon and the individual is unable to develop his own Water Carrier powers, he'll get corns. And so we can always use the human being as an instrument to see what is happening in the universe. We have to do it scientifically, however, and not from superstition. And so, in this way, it is a proper scientific method used in the science of the spirit. Of course, it is vague the way many people think it, and then one cannot see anything from what they are thinking. This is where the old maxim applies: when the cock on the midden crows, the weather will change or stay as it was. It is indeed exactly the way many people think about the world: when the cock on the midden crows, the weather will change or stay as it was.

But when we really go into the matter, that is no longer the case. Through the human being, the most perfect instrument you can have, you perceive things more perfectly than through anything else in the universe. So it is not a matter of simply inventing things, but you study what goes on in the human being. You need to know, of course, how it is with corns, how they develop out of the skin, and so on, and only then can you see what happens when the Water Carrier is covered up. But if we study the matter through the human being, we can study the whole universe through the human being.

19. The cultural epochs and the passage of the equinox

Rudolf Steiner frequently spoke of the great cultural epochs of 2160 years, which he dates from the destruction of Atlantis. These are also designated according to the constellations, depending on which one is rising at the spring equinox. He then relates these to the particular planets said to govern the constellation and from this makes very interesting observations, such as the connection between the moon, Cancer and the first post-Atlantean epoch, which he called the ancient Indian epoch in which there was an innocent and joyful relationship to sex, as can be seen from the surviving sculptures and myths. These periods can be broken down further into three decanates (3 × 10 degrees of a 30 degree sign), or periods of 720 years during which there is also an influence from another planet. The system of sub-rulerships is a traditional one which begins with Mars as the ruler of the first decanate of Aries, then follows the planetary sequence Jupiter, Saturn, moon, Mercury, Venus, sun, Mars, to the end of Pisces with Mars ruling the last decanate as in the diagram.

If we look at things rightly, we can say that, on one hand, it simply is the case that we live in the materialistic age, and that materialism necessarily leads to abstraction as we have come to know it: that is, the alienation from reality and all the catastrophic consequences in our time arising from this alienation from reality. On the other hand, it can also be said that of the various epochs in the post-Atlantean period, to talk only of these, our fifth epoch is in some respect the greatest age, the one that brings the most to humanity, one that harbours within it immense possibilities for the evolution and existence of humanity. And it is precisely through the things which human beings develop as the shadow side of spiritual life, precisely through those, that human beings make their way into the spiritual world if they proceed rightly. This will, in fact, be the path to the most authentic, the highest of human goals. Evolutionary possibilities in our time are great, greater in some ways than they were in former phases of post-Atlantean evolution. In point of fact, something of immense significance occurred with the beginning of this fifth post-Atlantean period. If we are to give the right colouring to and have the right nuance of feeling for some of the things we have repeatedly brought up from various viewpoints, we must look in a completely new way at the relationship between the human being and the universe. Of course, all those clever old alumni will call it superstition to speak of a connection between the human being and actual constellations in the cosmos. What matters is to understand that connection properly. Superstition—what is superstition? The belief that human beings must in some way take their bearings from the universe? We go by the clock, which we set by the position of the sun; every time we look at a clock, we practise astrology. There are subconscious parts of human nature that take their direction from constellations other than those we go by when in physical life we set our clocks by them. If things are understood rightly, it makes no sense at all to talk of superstition. By way of illustration, I shall now set before your soul a portion of this world-clock. We will use it to look further at the riddle that was raised earlier.

The first post-Atlantean cultural epoch arose after the flooding of Atlantis, when the flood which separates our culture from the Atlantean culture had receded. The macrocosmic influence on that period was such that the force flowing through earthly life was the one corresponding to the rising of the sun at the vernal equinox in the sign of Cancer. Thus we can say that when the sun entered the sign of Cancer at the vernal equinox the first post-Atlantean civilization began. It could actually be called the 'Cancer civilization' as long as we do not misunderstand the expression. In other words, when the sun rose in the spring it stood in the sign of Cancer.

We said earlier that something in the human being always corresponds to things out in the macrocosm. In the human being, Cancer corresponds to the thorax. Speaking in terms of the macrocosm, the first Indian culture was characterized by the fact that it occurred while the vernal equinox of the sun was in Cancer. If one were to characterize it from the per-spective of the microcosm, one could say that this Indian culture occurred at a time when human beings' knowledge of the world, their perceptions, their world-view were under the influence of those forces which in the Crab are expressed within the shell of its chest, within its cuirass. Physical human beings today cannot enter into a perceptive and sensitive relationship with the world through the forces of their 'Crab'. If human beings develop the forces that are intimately related to the thorax, if through their thorax they sense all that goes on in nature and in human life, then it will be as if they came into direct touch with the outer world, with all that approaches them from the elemental world. The relation between human beings that underlay the original Indian culture was such that if one human being encountered another, each felt the other's nature, as it were, through the sensitivity of the thorax. The other person was felt to be sympathetic or more or less

antipathetic. Just by breathing the air in a person's surroundings, one would learn to know that person. Modern
humanity knows nothing of this, and in some ways it is an
advantage. Still, we do each breathe differently in the
proximity of another person. For when we are in the proximity
of others, we breathe the air expired by them. Modern human
beings have become very insensitive to this. But in the Cancer
phase of the first post-Atlantean culture this insensitivity did
not exist. A human being could be perceived as sympathetic
or antipathetic through his or her breath. My own breath
would have moved differently depending on whether the
person was sympathetic or antipathetic. And my chest would
have been sensitive enough to be aware of its movements.

Just think what one actually perceived! One perceived the
other, but one perceived the other through something that
took place in oneself. People experienced the other person's
inwardness through a process that was perceived as one's
own inwardness, one's own bodily inwardness. This was the
Cancer culture, illustrated by the example of the meeting of
two human beings. But that was the way the whole world was
perceived. This was the foundation on which the first post-
Atlantean culture was built. A person breathed differently
when looking at the sun, when looking at the dawn, when
looking at spring, when looking at autumn; and from one's
breathing, concepts were derived. And just as modern
humanity forms its abstract, its strawlike abstract—not even
straw, its paper-like abstract—concepts of the sun, moon and
stars, of growth and blossoming, of everything imaginable, so
in the first post-Atlantean culture, the Cancer culture,
human beings formed concepts, but their concepts were felt
in this direct way, as co-vibrating with one's own Cancer,
one's thorax.

We can say, therefore, that if this represents the path of the sun, and the spring sun stands in Cancer, then this is the time when the human being also is in a Cancer culture.

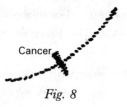

Fig. 8

Every constellation of the zodiac is related to a particular planet and must be regarded as belonging to that planet. (The reasons for this are probably known by most of you, but I will perhaps mention them presently.) Cancer is considered to be particularly connected to the moon. Since the forces of the moon work in a very particular way when it stands in Cancer, one says that the moon has its house, its home in Cancer. Its forces reside there, and there they are particularly developed.

Now, just as in the human being the thorax corresponds to Cancer, so does the sexual sphere correspond to the planetary moon. In fact one can say that, whereas on the one hand humans were so susceptible, so receptive and sensitive in the first post-Atlantean epoch, on the other hand all intimate aspects of the then world conception which have come to light are concerned precisely with the sexual sphere. At that time this was appropriate, for there was an innocence which disappeared in later, more corrupt ages.

Then the sun entered the sign of Gemini, the Twins, at the vernal equinox. As long as the vernal equinox continued to be in Gemini, we are dealing with the second, Persian, post-Atlantean cultural epoch. In the microcosmic realm, Gemini was expressed in all that concerns human symmetry, in particular the symmetrical relationship between right and left hand. There are of course other aspects of our being symmetrical; for instance, we see things singly with our two eyes. This cooperation between right and left, shown particularly in the hands and arms, corresponds in the macrocosm to Gemini.

Now that which the human being takes into life through the forces of Gemini, the forces of symmetry, with regard to his world-view (just as earlier things were taken in through the thorax) is less closely connected with the person's immediate surroundings. The fact of being symmetrical connects the human being more with what lies away from the earth—not the realm of the earth, but that of the heavens, the cosmic realm. Hence, in the second post-Atlantean epoch, the close connection with the immediate elemental surroundings of the earth fades away, and the Zarathustrian[69] culture appears. This culture was turned towards the Gemini nature in the world—on one hand to the nature of light, on the other hand to the nature of darkness, the twinned natures connected with the forces which the human being expresses through bodily symmetry.

Just as the moon has its house in Cancer, so Mercury has its house in Gemini (see diagram p. 231). And just as in the first post-Atlantean epoch the force of the sexual sphere helped the human being to form an intimate relationship with the surrounding world, so with the second post-Atlantean epoch help came from the sphere of Mercury, which is connected with the lower body. On the one hand, the human being's forces pass away from the earth into the outer universe, but in this, as it were, the human being is helped by something that is still heavily tinged with atavistic forces, that is, all that is connected with the vascular and digestive systems. The human digestive system is not just for the digestion of food, it is at the same time an instrument of knowledge. We have forgotten these things. And real judgement—not the 'feel' of which I have spoken earlier, but real discernment, the deeper gift for combination which creates connection with objects—does not come from the head, but from the lower body, and was of service during this second post-Atlantean period.

Then came the third age when the sun at the vernal equinox entered Taurus, the Bull. The forces that descend from the universe when the sun stands in Taurus at the spring equinox are connected in the human microcosm with the regions of the larynx, the forces of the larynx. Hence, in this third post-Atlantean epoch, the Egypto-Chaldean human beings developed as their special organ of knowledge all that is related to the larynx. The feeling of relationship between the spoken word and the object, the word and the things out in the universe, was especially strong in that time. These days, in the age of abstractions, it is not easy to form much of an idea of the intimate connection humans established with the cosmos as they knew it through their larynx.

In this case, the forces which correspond to Taurus were assisted by Venus, whose house is in Taurus (see diagram p. 231). In the human microcosm this corresponds to forces which lie between the heart and the stomach. So whatever was known in that time as the cosmic word was intimately connected with human beings, since the latter understood it through the forces of Venus residing in their own body.

There followed the Graeco-Latin time, the fourth post-Atlantean epoch. The sun entered Aries, the Ram, at the vernal equinox. In the human being, this corresponds to the head region, the region of the brow, the upper head. A time began during which humans mainly sought to grasp the world through understanding, and this relationship to the world led to thoughts. Head knowledge is very different from earlier forms of knowing. However, despite the fact that the head is an almost exact image of the macrocosm, and in fact precisely because in a physical sense it is an exact repro- duction of the macrocosm, it is really of very little value for spiritual purposes. Forgive me for saying so but, being of a physical nature, the human head is worth very little. And whenever human beings rely primarily on their head, all they can produce is an intellectual culture.

The Graeco-Latin time brought the head culture to a high point and thus gradually brought the human being into a special relationship with the universe, evolving gradually into a fully fledged head and thinking culture, which in turn ran its course and came to an end. So, from the fifteenth century onwards, as I pointed out yesterday, people were no longer able to connect thinking with reality. However, this head culture, this Aries culture, was such that the human being internalized the observation of the universe. As regards the physical world, this Aries culture was most welcome. Only in its decadent form has it became materialistic. The human being in this Aries civilization formed a special relationship with the surrounding world precisely through the head. It is particularly difficult today to understand Greek culture. Roman culture developed a more commonplace—philistine even—version of it, but we do not realize that, for instance, the Greeks' notion of concepts and ideas was different from ours. I have dealt with this in my *Riddles of Philosophy*.[70]

That Mars had its house in Aries was most significant for that age. Once again, the forces of Mars are connected with the nature of the human larynx, but in a different way, so Mars, who imparts aggressiveness, was particularly supportive of all that developed in the way of a relationship to the world through the head. In the fourth post-Atlantean era, from the eighth century BC to the fifteenth century AD, those conditions were developed which could be described as a Mars culture. The configuration of the social structures that spread over the earth during that time was primarily connected to a Mars culture, a warlike culture. Nowadays, wars are outdated. Although they may be more frightening, they are really stragglers. We shall come back to this.

Now, the human head with all its forces, and as a purely physical thinking tool, is an image of the starry heaven. For this reason there was still something macrocosmic in human thoughts in the fourth post-Atlantean time; thoughts were not yet bound up with the earth. But think now of the revolution that happened with the fifteenth century when the Aries culture passed over into Pisces. Pisces forces are those forces in the human being that are connected with the feet. There was a transition from head to feet; it was an immense shift. That is why, if you go back into the time before the fourteenth century with some understanding, and read the alchemical and other writings that are so despised today, you see what deep, what vast insights existed then about cosmic mysteries. But all of human culture—and human forces, too—was completely turned around. What humans had formerly received from the heavens they now received from the earth. The celestial constellations show us how great a shift had taken place in the human being. And this is connected with the beginning of the materialistic age. Thoughts lose their power, thoughts easily turn into empty phrases.

But now consider another remarkable thing. Just as Venus

dwells in Taurus and Mars in Aries, so Jupiter's house is in Pisces. And Jupiter is connected with the development of the human brow, the forehead. If the human being can rise to greatness in the fifth post-Atlantean period, it is precisely because, in the full independence of their humanity, human beings have become able to use the forces of their head to refine and encompass that which was brought to them from the other side. In other words, Jupiter performs the same service for humans in the fifth post-Atlantean epoch that Mars did in the fourth. In a certain respect one might say that Mars was king of this world in the fourth post-Atlantean epoch. But in the fifth, he is not the rightful king of this world because nothing can really be attained through Mars forces in the fifth post-Atlantean epoch. Rather, the greatness of this epoch must be brought about through the forces of the spiritual life, understanding of the world, perception of the world. Human beings are shut off from the heavenly forces, confined in the materialistic period. But in this fifth post-Atlantean age humans have the greatest opportunity of making themselves into beings of the spirit. No age has been as favourable to spirituality as this fifth epoch. All that is needed is the courage to drive the money-changers out of the Temple. This age must find the courage to set reality, the whole of reality and thus spiritual reality, against the abstractions, against things alienated from reality.

Those who read the stars have always known that particular planets affect various sections of the zodiacal path. There is some justification for assigning to each of these constellations—moon-Cancer, Mercury-Gemini, Venus-Taurus, Mars-Aries, Jupiter-Pisces—three decanates, as they are called. These three decanates represent those planets which have a particular mission during a particular con-

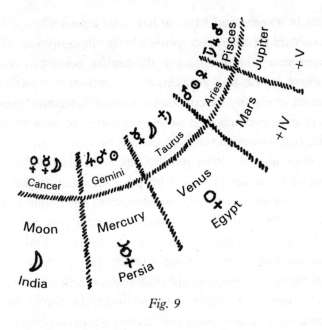

Fig. 9

stellation, while the others remain less active. Thus for the
first post-Atlantean age, the Cancer epoch, Venus, Mercury
and the moon are the decanates; during the Gemini epoch,
Jupiter, Mars, the sun; during the Taurus epoch, Mercury,
moon, Saturn; during the Aries epoch, Mars, sun, Venus.
During our own age, the age of Pisces, the characteristic
decanates, the forces that can serve us the most according to
the celestial clock are Saturn, Jupiter and Mars. Mars,
working here differently from when it was in its own house in
Aries, is now the representative of human strength. In the
outer planets, with Saturn and Jupiter, Mars[71] is connected
with the human head, the human countenance, word formation. Thus all that is connected with spirituality for this
life between birth and death is especially serviceable in this
epoch. This epoch contains the greatest spiritual possibilities.
In no other age was it granted to human beings to do as much

wrong as in this age, in no other age could one sin more seriously against the inner mission of the time. Anyone living in consonance with the age will use the Jupiter force to transform the forces coming from the earth into a spiritually free humanity. And we have at our disposal the best, the finest powers developed by human beings between birth and death: the Saturn, Jupiter and Mars forces.

The world-clock is favourable to this age, but we cannot afford to be fatalistic about things. People must not say, 'Well, let us leave things to world destiny, everything is sure to come right.' Instead, it gives people who have the will to do so—but they must have the will—the opportunity to discover endless possibilities in our age. Only, as yet, people have not given much evidence that they do have the will.

But neither is there any reason for saying, 'Well, what can I do by myself? The world is just taking its course.' And certainly the world is not paying any attention to us now. But the point I wish to make is a different one. Unlike people 33 years ago we cannot say that we will not bother ourselves about anything, for that is the way we arrived at our current predicament. The point for our time is that each person individually should begin to want to escape from abstraction, to lay aside what is alienated from reality and to seek—each person himself—to approach reality and get beyond abstraction.

We must move away from far-fetched concepts if we are to develop the important matters that will occupy us in the next few days: discussion of the ageing of the human being, that is, the going-towards-death as much as the coming-from-birth. Today education, the practical education of children, proceeds entirely from a total concentration on the fact that the child is born and develops as a child; but the time must come when the child also learns what it means to become older. It is not at all easy to develop these things. We need to reach further for the necessary concepts. Let us put it this way: to overcome the estrangement from reality, which is the signature of our time, it is of the utmost importance for human beings to develop the will to be attentive, that is, the will to set Jupiter in motion. For that precisely is Jupiter's nature: it is the force that makes a perpetual call on our attentiveness.

20. Michael and the manifestation of the divine spiritual

Towards the latter part of his activity Steiner spoke more frequently about the spiritual being of Michael, formerly an archangel and now a member of the Archai or hierarchy of Time Spirits, but still also fulfilling archangelic functions. Archangels rule historical periods of approximately 350 years, which also have a planetary connection, namely: 550–200 BCE Michael (Sun); 200 BCE–150 CE Oriphiel (Saturn); 150–500 Anael (Venus); 500–850 Zachariel (Jupiter); 850–1190 Raphael (Mercury); 1190–1510 Samael (Mars); 1510–1879 Gabriel (Moon); 1879–2230 approx. Michael (Sun).[72] Thus Michael is the ruler of the present age. In this letter to the members of the Anthroposophical Society written near the end of his life, Steiner points out that we are now within a finished creation or 'wrought work', and a certain separation has come about between this and the creative spiritual beings. It is however due to Michael that there can still be a living connection, a harmony between human beings and the stars, but most remarkably this is because human beings themselves seek it and so Michael works through them to maintain it.

Following this extract is a verse, which Steiner wrote for his wife, the speech artist Marie Steiner von Sivers, which exemplifies the manner in which he hoped human beings would continue to respond.

How does the human being stand today in his present stage of evolution with respect to Michael and his hosts?

The human being is surrounded today by a world which

was once of a wholly divine spiritual nature—of a divine spiritual being of which he also was a member. Thus at that time the world belonging to the human being was a world of divine spiritual being. But this was no longer so in a later stage of evolution. The world had then become a cosmic manifestation of the divine spiritual; the divine being hovered behind the manifestation. Nevertheless, the divine spiritual lived and moved in all that was thus manifested. A world of stars was already there, in the light and movement of which the divine spiritual lived and moved and manifested itself. One may say that at that time, in the position or movement of a star, the activity of the divine and spiritual was directly evident.

And in all this—in the working of the divine spirit in the cosmos, and in the life of the human being resulting from this divine activity—Michael was as yet in his own element, unhindered, unresisted. The adjustment of the relation between the divine and the human was in his hands.

But other ages dawned. The world of the stars ceased to be a direct and present manifestation of divine spiritual activity. The constellations lived and moved, maintaining what the divine activity had been in them in the past. The divine spiritual dwelt in the cosmos in revelation no longer, but in the manner of its working only. There was now a certain distinct separation between the divine spiritual and the cosmic world. Michael, by virtue of his own nature, adhered to the divine spiritual, and endeavoured to keep humankind as closely as possible in touch with it.

This he continued to do, more and more. His will was to preserve the human being from living too intensely in a world which represents only the working of the divine and spiritual—which is not the real being, nor its manifestation.

It is a deep source of satisfaction to Michael that through the human being himself he has succeeded in keeping the world of the stars in direct union with the divine and spiritual. For when the human being, having fulfilled his life between death and a new birth, enters on the way to a new earth life, in his descent he seeks to establish a harmony between the course of the stars and his coming life on earth. In olden times this harmony existed as a matter of course, because the divine spiritual was active in the stars, where human life too had its source. But today, when the course of the stars is only a continuation of the manner in which the divine spiritual worked in the past, this harmony could not exist unless the human being sought it. The human being brings his divine spiritual portion—which he has preserved from the past—into relation with the stars, which now only bear their divine spiritual nature within them as something working from an earlier time.

In this way there comes into the human being's relation to the world something of the divine, which corresponds to former ages and yet appears in these later times. That this is so, is the deed of Michael. And this deed gives him such deep satisfaction that in it he finds a portion of his very life, a portion of his sun-like, living energy.

> Stars once spoke to us,
> their silence now is world destiny;
> awareness of this silence
> can cause us earthly human beings pain.
>
> But in mute stillness ripens
> what we speak to the stars;
> awareness of this speech
> can strengthen our spiritual core.[73]

Notes

1. *The Philosophy of Spiritual Activity, a Philosophy of Freedom (Intuitive Thinking as a Spiritual Path)* (GA 4) (London: Rudolf Steiner Press, 1992) and others.
2. Dornach 17 February 1924, *Karmic Relationships*, Vol. 1, tr. G. Adams (GA 235) (London: Rudolf Steiner Press, 1972).
3. Elisabeth Vreede, *Astronomy and Spiritual Science. The Astronomical Letters of Elisabeth Vreede*, Year 2, Letter 2, October 1928, 'The Nature of Astrology', tr. R. Koetzsch and A. Riegel (Great Barrington, MA: SteinerBooks, 2009).
4. Rudolf Grosse, *The Christmas Foundation; beginning of a New Cosmic Age*, tr. J. Collis (N. Vancouver: Steiner Book Centre, 1984).
5. See Note 3, Year 2 Letter 1, September 1928, 'When Mercury Stood in Libra'.
6. Heinz Walther, 'Towards a New Astrology', *The Modern Mystic*, October 1939, quoting Rudolf Steiner, *Christ and the Spiritual World*, Leipzig, 2 January 1914, tr. C. Davy and D. S. Osmond (GA 149) (London: Rudolf Steiner Press 1983).
7. Heinz Walther, 'Towards a New Astrology', *The Modern Mystic*, October 1939.
8. Maria and Matthias Thun, *The Biodynamic Sowing and Planting Calendar* (Edinburgh: Floris Books, 2009).
9. Lili Kolisko, *Gold and the Sun*, Kolisko Archive 1947, *Jupiter and Tin*, Stuttgart 1932, *The Working of Stars in Earthly Substances*, Stuttgart 1928, *The Agriculture of Tomorrow*, Kolisko Archive 1978 (with E. Kolisko).
10. Nick Kollerstrom, *Gardening & Planting by the Moon. Higher Yields in Vegetables & Flowers* (Slough: Quantum, 2008). Robert Powell: *History of the Zodiac* (San Rafael, CA: Sophia Academic Press, 2007).

11. Alexander Thom, *Megalithic Lunar Observatories* (Oxford: Oxford University Press, 1973).

12. Berne, 6 September 1910, *The Gospel of St. Matthew*, tr. D.S. Osmond and M. Kirkaldy (GA 123) (London: Rudolf Steiner Press, 1965).

13. Vienna 10 April 1914, *The Inner Nature of Man*, tr. A.R. Meuss (GA 153) (London: Rudolf Steiner Press, 1994).

14. Dornach 10 February 1923, *Earthly Knowledge and Heavenly Wisdom*, tr. S. Seiler (GA 221) (Hudson, NY: Anthroposophic Press, 1991).

15. Elisabeth Vreede, Astronomical Letters, published as *Astronomy and Spiritual Science* (see note 3).

16. Akasha Chronicle: a spiritual record of all human deeds.

17. Johann Wolfgang von Goethe (1749–1832), *The Metamorphosis of Plants*.

18. Johannes Kepler, astronomer (1571–1630), Albrecht Duke of Wallenstein (1583–1634).

19. Shakespeare, *Hamlet*, Act 1, Scene 5.

20. Tycho Brahe, Danish astronomer (1546–1601).

21. *Educating Children Today (Education of the Child)*, tr. revised by M. Barton (GA 34) (Forest Row: Rudolf Steiner Press, 2008).

22. Wilhelm Fliess, Berlin doctor (1858–1928), an early proponent of biorhythms.

23. Nostradamus or Michel de Nostradame (1503–1566). For 1999 see *Centuries*, 10:72.

24. Goethe, *Die Weissagen des Bakis* (The Soothsayings of Bakis), 1798 (*Goethe's Tragi-Comic Observations on Life, Time, History*, tr. H. Jantz, Baltimore: Johns Hopkins Press, 1966).

25. See for instance *The Gospel of St Matthew* (see note 12), and *The Gospel of St Luke* (GA 114) (London: Rudolf Steiner Press, 1988).

26. The Rose Cross is the emblem of the Rosicrucians. Tradition associates the rose with Persia, the cross is the symbol of Christianity. Historically the Rosicrucian Order is thought to

have been founded as a secret society *c.* 1430 by Christian Rosenkreutz, and is commonly associated with healing, occultism, alchemy. Steiner counters the '... materialistic caricature of Rosicrucianism ... presented today. The task of the Rosicrucians was to formulate a science by means of which they would be able to let their (universal) wisdom flow gradually into the world' (*Rosicrucian Esotericism,* Spring Valley, NY: Anthroposophic Press, 1978). See also George Adams, *The Mysteries of the Rose-Cross* (London: Temple Lodge, 1989).

27. Gnosticism arose in the Hellenistic era. Gnostics believed that salvation is attained through knowledge rather than through faith or deeds.

28. Arius (*c.* 250–336), Greek ecclesiastic at Alexandria. Taught Neoplatonic doctrine that God is alone, unknowable, and separate from every created being, that Christ is a created being and not God in the fullest sense but a secondary deity, and that in the incarnation the Logos assumed a body but not a human soul. Growing dispute over his teaching led Emperor Constantine to call the Council of Nicaea (325) where Arianism was declared heresy.
Saint Athanasius (*c.* 293-373), Greek theologian and prelate in Egypt. Lifelong opponent of Arianism. Attended Council of Nicaea (325) as deacon. Bishop of Alexandria. Advocated homoousian doctrine. Often exiled because of his opposition to Arianism. Wrote doctrinal works. Not author of Athanasian creed, which originated later (fifth or sixth century).

29. Johann Wolfgang von Goethe (1749–1832), leading German poet and playwright. *Faust* (1808–32), a drama in verse, is Goethe's masterpiece. The lines referred to are in Part Two, Scene 2.

30. Nathan and Solomon were both sons of King David, the second king of Israel. The Gospel of St Luke cites Nathan as a forefather of Mary (Luke 3:31); St Matthew traces Joseph's

lineage to Solomon (Matthew 1:16). For a detailed account of the two Jesus children, see Rudolf Steiner, *From Jesus to Christ* (London: Rudolf Steiner Press, 1973), lecture 8.

31. The Zoroaster mentioned here by Steiner lived in very ancient times, according to the Greeks—already 5000 years before the Trojan War. He is not identical with the Zoroaster or Zarathustra mentioned in ordinary history.

32. Buddha, Indian religious leader, founder of Buddhism. Historical name Siddhartha Gautama, *c.* 563–483 BC. Some eastern religions believe him one of the last incarnations of the Godhead. Son of a royal family, he renounced luxury and became an ascetic.

    Bodhisattva, a being that compassionately refrains from entering Nirvana for the salvation of others.

33. Steiner describes the human being as comprised of four 'bodies': physical, etheric, astral, and ego. The astral body bears the inner world of desires, pleasure and pain, and the qualitative world of emotions. See *Occult Science*.

34. Nicolaus Copernicus (1473–1543), Polish astronomer. Made astronomical observations of orbits of sun, moon, planets. Gradually abandoned accepted Ptolemaic system of astronomy and worked out heliocentric system in which the earth rotates daily on its axis and, with other planets, revolves around the sun.

35. Giordano Bruno (1548–1600), Italian philosopher. Arrested by the Inquisition and burned at the stake. A critic of Aristotelian logic and champion of Copernican cosmology, which he extended with the notion of the infinite universe.

36. Nicholas Cusanus (1401–1464), German prelate and philosopher. Bishop, subsequently created cardinal. Wrote treatises for Church Councils as well as works on mathematics and philosophy. Anticipated Copernicus by his belief in the earth's rotation and revolution around the sun.

    Galileo Galilei (1564–1642), Italian mathematician,

astronomer, and physicist. First to use a telescope to study the skies. Tried by the Inquisition for supporting the Copernican system.

37. See note 21.

38. The change from the old idea of the earth at the centre to one in which the earth and planets revolve around the sun. For a fuller understanding and the consequence to the planets Venus and Mercury, see *Spiritual Hierarchies and the Physical World*, Düsseldorf 12–18 April 1909, with the appendix by Georg Unger (Hudson, NY: Anthroposophic Press 1996).

39. See Chapter 19 for a fuller explanation of the cultural epochs.

40. Joachim Schultz, *Movement and Rhythm of the Stars*, tr. J. Meeks (Edinburgh: Floris Books, 1986).

41. Slightly abridged from 'Wise Jupiter' by Margaret Jonas, The Astrological Association *Journal*, Jan/Feb 1988.

42. Contrary to the conventional classification, Steiner here includes Mars with the outer planets.

43. Steiner described the period dating from the fifteenth century as of the consciousness or spiritual soul, which means that humanity would develop more independent objective soul forces.

44. *Knowledge of the Higher Worlds (How to Know Higher Worlds)* (GA 10) (London: Rudolf Steiner Press, 1993).

45. *Occult Science—an Outline (An Outline of Esoteric Science)* (GA 13) (London: Rudolf Steiner Press, 1979).

46. It does not follow that because lunar explorations have not revealed physical life that there is no spiritual life.

47. Pluto was not discovered until 1932.

48. We should not assume that the nature of the planet is entirely synonymous with the attributes of the Graeco-Roman goddess, though it is of interest to note that the goddess was said to have taken the smith-god Vulcan as her lover—very much an earth spirit.

49. See note 38.

50. Monistic Union: founded in Jena in 1906 under the honorary chairmanship of the scientist Ernst Haeckel (1834–1919).
51. Felix Balde: a character in Steiner's *Four Mystery Dramas*, tr. H. and R. Pusch (GA 14) (London: Rudolf Steiner Press, 1997). See especially Scenes 5 and 6 of *The Soul's Awakening*.
52. See Steiner, *The Gospel of St Luke*, tr. D.S. Osmond (GA 114) (London: Rudolf Steiner Press, 1988).
53. Francis of Assisi (1182–1226). See Steiner, *The Spiritual Foundation of Morality*, tr. M. Gardner (GA 155) (Hudson, NY: Anthroposophic Press, 1995.
54. Raphael Sanzio (1483–1520), reincarnation of John the Baptist, see Steiner, 'The Last Address', *Karmic Relationships*, Vol. 4 (GA 238) (London: Rudolf Steiner Press, 1997). Also lecture of 30 January 1913, 'The Mission of Raphael' (GA 62), typescript translation Z 27 (Rudolf Steiner House Library).
55. Leonardo da Vinci (1452–1519). Lecture in Berlin, 13 February 1913 (GA 62), typescript translation p. 31.
56. See *Education for Special Needs*, tr. M. Adams (GA 317) (London: Rudolf Steiner Press, 1998), with an introduction by Albrecht Strohschein on the beginning of special needs education within anthroposophy.
57. *Theosophy* (GA 9), tr. M. Cotterell (London: Rudolf Steiner Press, 1989) and C. Creeger (Hudson, NY: Anthroposophic Press, 1994).
58. See note 3.
59. See note 56.
60. The original leader of the Mathematical Astronomical Section at the Goetheanum.
61. Willi Sucher, *Isis Sophia III—Our Relationship with the Stars* (Weobley: Anastasi Ltd., 2000).
62. See note 23.
63. Except for circumpolar stars.
64. See note 20.

65. Ptolemy or Claudius Ptolemaeus (*c.* AD 87–165), Egyptian geographer, mathematician and astronomer.

66. Edmund Halley (1656–1742), English astronomer.

67. Translator's note: this is the phrase Rudolf Steiner used.

68. Paris, 25 May–14 June 1906, in *An Esoteric Cosmology* (GA 94) (Blauvelt: Garber Communications, 1987). The summaries by E. Schuré do not include Steiner's statements concerning the comet atmosphere.

69. The age of the spiritual teacher Zarathustra, *c.* 6000 BC, and later incarnations. (See also note 12.)

70. *Riddles of Philosophy* (GA 18) (Spring Valley, NY: Anthroposophic Press, 1973).

71. See note 42.

72. Torquay, 18 August 1924, *True and False Paths in Spiritual Investigation*, tr. A.H. Parker (GA 243) (London: Rudolf Steiner Press, 1985).

73. *Breathing the Spirit. Meditations for Times of Day and Seasons of the Year*, tr. M. Barton (from GA 40, 267, 268) (Forest Row: Rudolf Steiner Press, 2007).

Sources

1. How does theosophy regard astrology
'How Does Theosophy Regard Astrology?', essay from 1905 in *Luzifer-Gnosis* (GA 34) (Dornach: Rudolf Steiner Verlag, 1987), tr. for this volume by Christian von Arnim

2. Prophecy: its nature and meaning
Lecture, Berlin, 9 November 1911, tr. D.S. Osmond, in *Prophecy, Its Nature and Meaning* (GA 61) (London: Anthroposophical Publishing Co., 1950)

3. Cosmic influences on the individual and humanity
Lecture, Copenhagen, 8 June 1911, tr. by S. Desch, in *The Spiritual Guidance of the Individual and Humanity* (GA 15) (Hudson, NY: Anthroposophic Press, 1992). Extract

4. The subtle impact of the stars
Lecture, Dornach, 3 December 1922, tr. D.S. Osmond, in *Man and the World of Stars and the Spiritual Communion of Mankind* (GA 219) (Spring Valley, NY: Anthroposophic Press, 1982). Extract

5. The human being as expression of the constellations and the planets
Lectures, Christiania (Oslo), 7 and 11 June 1912, tr. unknown, in *Man in the Light of Occultism, Theosophy and Philosophy* (GA 137) (London: Rudolf Steiner Press, 1964). Extracts

6. Understanding the human form out of the universe
Lecture, Dornach 28 October 1921, tr. A.R. Meuss, in *Cosmosophy*, Vol. 2 (GA 208) (Lower Beechmont, Australia: Completion Press, 1997)

7. The changing vision of the universe
'The bridge between universal spirituality and the physical con-

stitution of the human being', Dornach, 18 December 1920, tr. revised by G.F. Karnow, in *Course for Young Doctors* (GA 202) (Chestnut Ridge, NY: Mercury Press, 1994). Extract

8. The forces of the planets
Lecture, 5 May 1921, tr. M. St Goar, in *Materialism and the Task of Anthroposophy* (GA 204) (Spring Valley, NY: Anthoposophic Press, 1987). Extract

9. The spiritual individualities of the planets
'The Spiritual Individualities of the Planets' (GA 228), Dornach, 27 July 1923, in *Golden Blade* 1988

10. The human being's inner cosmic system
'The human being's inner cosmic system', Prague, 23 March 1911, in *An Occult Physiology* (GA 128) (London: Rudolf Steiner Press, 1983). Extract

11. The planetary spheres and life between death and rebirth
Lectures, Munich, 12 March 1913 and 26 November 1912, tr. M. Querido, in *Life Between Death and Rebirth* (GA 140) (Spring Valley, NY: Anthoposophic Press, 1978). Extracts

12. The spiritual preparation of the human body between death and a new birth
Lecture, Christiania (Oslo), 17 May 1923, tr. E. McArthur, in *Man's Being, His Destiny and World Evolution* (GA 226) (Spring Valley, NY: Anthroposophic Press, 1984). Extract

13. The human being and his pattern in the stars
Lecture, Berlin, 26 March 1918, tr. C. Davy and D.S. Osmond, in *Earthly Death and Cosmic Life* (GA181) (London: Rudolf Steiner Press, 1964). Extract

14. The forces of the earth and the constellation at birth in determining human characteristics
Lectures, Dornach, 5 and 6 July 1924, tr. M. Adams, in *Education*

for Special Needs (GA 317) (London: Rudolf Steiner Press, 1998). Extracts

15. The revelation of the stars at death
Lecture, Dornach, 21 January 1917, tr. J. Collis, in *The Karma of Untruthfulness*, Vol. 2 (GA 174) (Forest Row: Rudolf Steiner Press, 2005). Extract

16. Human and cosmic rhythms
Lecture, Dornach, 16 April 1920, tr. revised by M. Barton, in *Mystery of the Universe* (GA 201) (Forest Row: Rudolf Steiner Press, 2001). Extract

17. Solar and lunar eclipses
Lecture, Dornach, 25 June 1922, tr. V. Compton-Burnett, C. Davy, D.S. Osmond, K. Wegener, in *Human Questions and Cosmic Answers* (GA 213) (London: Anthroposophical Publishing Co., 1960). Extract

18. Comets and other cosmic phenomena
Lecture, Dornach, 17 May 1924, tr. A.R. Meuss, in *From Beetroot to Buddhism* (GA 353) (London: Rudolf Steiner Press, 1999)

19. The cultural epochs and the passage of the equinox
Lecture, Dornach, 8 January 1918, tr. M. Cotterell, revised M. Spiegler, in *Ancient Myths* (GA 180) (Hudson, NY: Anthroposophic Press, 1994). Extract

20. Michael and the manifestation of the divine spiritual
Anthroposophical Leading Thoughts: The Michael Mystery, 2 November 1924, tr. G. and M. Adams (GA 26) (London: Rudolf Steiner Press, 1973). Extract
Verse: 'Stars Once Spoke to Us', from *Breathing the Spirit*, tr. M. Barton (Forest Row: Rudolf Steiner Press, 2002)

Suggested further reading

Rudolf Steiner (in addition to those cited in the text)

The Relation of the Diverse Branches of Natural Science to Astronomy; *Third Scientific Lecture Course*, Typescript translation by G. Adams, R 81 (GA 232) (Rudolf Steiner House Library, London)

Spiritual Hierarchies and the Physical World, Düsseldorf, 12–18 April 1909, tr. R. Querido (GA 110) (Hudson, NY: Anthroposophic Press, 1996)

Spiritual Beings in the Heavenly Bodies and the Kingdoms of Nature, Helsingfors, 3–14 April 1912 (GA 136) (Hudson, NY: Anthroposophic Press, 1992)

Human and Cosmic Thought, Berlin, 20–23 January 1914, tr. C. Davy (GA 151) (London: Rudolf Steiner Press, 1991)

Eurythmy as Visible Speech, Dornach, 24 June–12 July 1924 (GA 279) (London: Anthroposophical Publishing Co., 1956)

The Riddle of Humanity [12 Senses and 7 Life Processes], Dornach, 29 July–3 September 1916, tr. J. Logan (GA 170) (London : Rudolf Steiner Press, 1990)

The Mystery of the Trinity, London, 30 August 1922 (GA 214) (Hudson, NY: Anthroposophic Press, 1991)

Agriculture, Koberwitz, 7–16 June 1924, tr. C. Creeger (Kimberton: Biodynamic Farming & Gardening Assoc. Inc., 1993)

From Sunspots to Strawberries, Dornach, 30 June–24 September 1924, revised by M. Barton (GA 354) (Forest Row: Rudolf Steiner Press, 2002)

Other authors

Elisabeth Vreede, *Astronomy and Spiritual Science [Astronomical Letters]*, tr. R. Koetzsch and A. Riegel (Great Barrington, MA: SteinerBooks, 2009)

Willi Sucher, *Cosmic Christianity and the Changing Countenance of Cosmology* (Great Barrington, MA: SteinerBooks, 1993)
Willi Sucher, *Isis Sophia I–III* (Weobley: Anastasi Ltd.)
Willi Sucher, *The Living Universe and the New Millennium* (Weobley: Anastasi Ltd.)
Hazel Straker, *Introductions to a Quest for a New Star Wisdom— Astrosophy* (Weobley: Anastasi Ltd.)
Joachim Schultz, *Movement and Rhythm of the Stars* (Edinburgh: Floris Books, 1986)
Norman Davidson, *Sky Phenomena. A Guide to Naked Eye Observation of the Heavens* (Edinburgh: Floris Books, 1993)
Frits H. Julius, *The Imagery of the Zodiac* (Edinburgh: Floris Books, 1993)

Other researchers include Robert Powell, David Tresemer and others. See Rudolf Steiner Press *www.rudolfsteinerpress.com*.

Note on Rudolf Steiner's Lectures

The lectures and addresses contained in this volume have been translated from the German, which is based on stenographic and other recorded texts that were in most cases never seen or revised by the lecturer. Hence, due to human errors in hearing and transcription, they may contain mistakes and faulty passages. Every effort has been made to ensure that this is not the case. Some of the lectures were given to audiences more familiar with anthroposophy; these are the so-called 'private' or 'members' lectures. Other lectures, like the written works, were intended for the general public. The difference between these, as Rudolf Steiner indicates in his *Autobiography*, is twofold. On the one hand, the members' lectures take for granted a background in and commitment to anthroposophy; in the public lectures this was not the case. At the same time, the members' lectures address the concerns and dilemmas of the members, while the public work arises from, and directly addresses Steiner's own understanding of universal needs. Nevertheless, as Rudolf Steiner stresses: 'Nothing was ever said that was not solely the result of my direct experience of the growing content of anthroposophy. There was never any question of concessions to the prejudices and preferences of the members. Whoever reads these privately printed lectures can take them to represent anthroposophy in the fullest sense. Thus it was possible without hesitation—when the complaints in this direction became too persistent—to depart from the custom of circulating this material "For members only". But it must be borne in mind that faulty passages do occur in these reports not revised by myself.' Earlier in the same chapter, he states: 'Had I been able to correct them [*the private lectures*], the restriction *for members only* would have been unnecessary from the beginning.' The original German editions on which this text is based were published by Rudolf Steiner Verlag, Dornach, Switzerland in the collected edition (*Gesamtausgabe*, 'GA') of Rudolf Steiner's work. All publications are edited by the Rudolf Steiner Nachlassverwaltung (estate), which wholly owns both Rudolf Steiner Verlag and the Rudolf Steiner Archive.